D0840707

VALUE OF CAMP

VALUE
of
CAMP

WALT BROCK

Iron Sharpeneth Iron Publications
Newberry Springs, California

VALUE OF CAMP
published by Iron Sharpeneth Iron Publications

© 2012 by Walt Brock

ISBN 978-193178730-7

LOC 2012953617

Unless otherwise noted, Scripture quotations are from the
Authorized King James Version.

Printed in the United States of America

ALL RIGHTS RESERVED.

No part of this book may be reproduced, stored in a retrieval system, or
transmitted, in any form or by any means—electronic or mechanical,
photocopying, recording, or otherwise—without prior written permission
from the Publisher. Inquiries should be addressed to Iron Sharpeneth
Iron Publications, 49191 Cherokee Road, Newberry Springs,
California 92365.

Managing Editor, Betty Brock

Book Design, Laura Lundy

Iron Sharpeneth Iron Publications
A ministry of Ironwood
Newberry Springs, California

CONTENTS

CHAPTER SEVEN   91
Market Factor in Determining Value of Camp

CHAPTER EIGHT   101
Reflections on the Value of Camp

APPENDIX A   113
Planning and Running a Week of Camp

APPENDIX B   116
The Spiritual Punch at Camp

ACKNOWLEDGMENTS

So many people have contributed time and effort to this little book that it seems a long list of authors would be appropriate instead of just one. The book has truly been a team endeavor and the culmination of many people's expertise, ideas, and suggestions—each one adding their unique skill and insight to the final product.

My son Sam, the Director of Ironwood, was perceptive and recognized the need for a document laying out the value of the camp ministry for both church leadership and the Christian family at a time when resources are scarce and traditional practices are being evaluated for their effectiveness with the goal of efficiency. I thank him for his encouragement to address the issue and for making it possible for many Ironwood team members to spend time and effort on the project.

I thank my talented and encouraging wife for her labor and support throughout the process. Her wise editing and rewrites have been done with much patience and skill—patience in starting over again from a different perspective and skill in shepherding this book through its many phases. There is no doubt in my mind this book would never have happened without her insight, labor, skill, and creativity.

With this project and several other Ironwood writing projects, Linda Phillips has given of herself in a labor of love as the primary editor of the first rough draft. The readers can add their thanks as well since she was merciless in cutting the unnecessary and eliminating the redundant. Thank you, Linda, for working with the deadlines we requested and skillfully challenging my verbosity without undermining the meaning.

I thank Beth Hunter for handling the in-house draft editions for the many camp leaders who read, commented, and suggested ways to improve over these three years. Their comments were invaluable to the process. Thanks as well to the Ironwood summer staff and resident staff teams for supplying the many illustrations and stories of how camp works to advance the cause of Christ. Also, my thanks goes to Emily Dickman for her work on the chapter summaries and Laura Lundy for the layout work.

I appreciate the Ironwood Board of Directors for allowing me to spend the time and energy on a project designed from the beginning to benefit many others camps besides our own—especially our camp co-laborers ministering all over the United States and gathering together every two years at the Tweakage Rendezvous. I trust this will become a valuable tool for each of their camping ministries.

I have endeavored to write this book from a philosophical bent that will apply to all Bible-believing camp ministries, but I must also acknowledge that the Ironwood philosophy of camp ministry will be evident as one reads this book. That being said, I acknowledge the value of any program philosophy of the camp ministry that adheres to the basics of the camp ministry outlined herein as the HEART of camping. My desire is that the contents of this book will encourage churches and families to diligently use this valuable method of reaching young people for the Lord Jesus Christ, strengthening families, and serving churches.

Lastly I must thank God Almighty for calling me into this ministry, providing for the needs of the ministry and my family, and allowing me the longevity of years to add a generational perspective to the wisdom and insight that comes from above. To God be the glory, great things He has not only done, but is as yet doing, and will keep on doing.

"Until Then!" your most grateful co-laborer in the work of the Lord,

Walt Brock
Co-founder of Ironwood

1 John 2:17

Endeavoring to do in time that which lasts for eternity.

INTRODUCTION

"Is camp worth it?" Yes, it is, and here is how I came to that conclusion.

While serving as a youth pastor in a large church in the West several decades ago, I planned, organized, and led the camps and retreats. Part of my leadership responsibilities included an evaluation of camp each year and a determination of what to do the next year. I had been given instructions by the church leadership that if I wanted to take our young people to camp, I would need to rent a facility, lead all of the activities, and use our church members as counselors. So, that is what I did. As I would evaluate each year, the work involved in doing camp right seemed overwhelming and just too excessive. But as I also evaluated the spiritual outcome of our efforts in reaching and teaching our young people, I became convinced, and remain so to this day, that the real reason the camp methodology was worth it was that young people made spiritual decisions at camp that changed their lives. Something about camp seemed to touch their hearts in a way that facilitated those decisions being made. Seeing the results of that heart change kept me going back for more. "Is camp worth it?" Absolutely!

Our church invested time, energy, and finances in our young people because they were important to us. When I look back on it now, some good camps may have been available to us, but we did not know of them. We chose a facility with similar biblical foundations, rented their facility, and handled the planning and operation. Each year I asked myself if I really wanted to do that to myself again. What was involved in the planning? I wrote out a list of twenty-two major items that I personally needed to do to run an effective camp program for our youth each summer. I noted only four items on the list that would be my responsibility if our church were to use a full-service camp. When I looked at the value of camp from that perspective, camp became more valuable to our ministry when we did not have to do all the preparation work and be responsible for executing the plans and programs. Camp was more valuable because the real cost to us in terms of time and effort was less, but the results were the same. Realizing this left me with a second answer to the same question, "Is camp worth it?" Absolutely!

This answer changed the direction of my life as I realized the value of a full-service camp ministry for our church and for other smaller churches that could not provide camp as our church had done. God burdened my heart to start a camp for similar churches looking for the kind of camping ministry we were doing with our own young people. Today, as a director of a camp for almost forty years, I have seen God use the methodology of camp in a harvest of decisions as He has given the increase. Amazingly, the answer is still the same, "Yes, camp is worth it!" Why? Let Jesus answer you . . .

> *Even so it is not the will of your Father which is in heaven, that one of these little ones should perish. Matthew 18:14*

> *For what is a man profited, if he shall gain the whole world, and lose his own soul? or what shall a man give in exchange for his soul? Matthew 16:26*

Walt Brock

One is worth more than all.

CHAPTER ONE
Camp—A Tool of the Church and Family

An Effective Tool

One constant in today's culture is the continuous drumbeat for change! While today we may feel threatened by high gas prices reducing our mobility, my own dad grew up on a Texas farm going to town once a month in a horse-drawn wagon. Most children today grow up with expectations of normalcy unheard of or reserved only for the very wealthy just one generation ago. So when we live in a society constantly changing and looking for bigger and better things, how do ministries reach both youth and adults with a constant and absolute message?

Living in a world full of "spectaculars" can be very daunting for any youth leader trying to compete with the bigger-and-better syndrome infecting our current society, but such a mentality is not the way to reach our young people today. Majoring only on the fun quotient, the world almost always outdoes any church youth group activity, especially if measured by the world's standards. To help with this struggle, the Lord has raised up a ministry designed to serve the local church and strengthen families "for such a time as this" *(Esther 4:14)*. It is a ministry specializing in fun and adventure, but not to the exclusion of emphasizing the necessity of living a Christ-like life. Intentionally designed to counter the busy lifestyle and mental clutter filling the minds of young and old alike, the camp ministry seeks to follow Christ's example of reaching people by presenting God's truth and allowing them to make decisions based on those truths. Camp is not the only tool in the youth leader's or pastor's toolbox of methods for reaching his youth group or congregation, but it is a very effective and efficient ministry tool when used to its fullest potential.

A Specialty Tool

In my woodshop, I have two drill presses. One is a relatively new Delta floor model, and the other is an old-fashioned bench top drill press made by Rockwell—a pre-World War II model out of my father's garage. It has less power and a much smaller capacity, but when I go to use a drill press, I almost always go to the old one unless a special need requires the larger, newer, more powerful one. I often wonder if I

> " My wife and I appreciate the time to sit back and evaluate our commitment to our Lord, our family, and each other. Thank you for the excellent preaching and for the example of what a servant should be.

16

wasted my money buying the new Delta drill press, but once in a while a task comes along requiring a serious drill press, and only the Delta can do the job. Therefore, I realize I did not waste money on purchasing it. Specialty tools are used less often but are absolutely essential to do certain jobs. Without such tools, I cannot complete certain projects.

The camp ministry is in many ways like that specialty tool. It is not used every day in ministry by a particular church or family but has great value because it accomplishes what often cannot be accomplished at home. People may wonder if it is worth the cost, time, or effort to use a camp ministry. To help with this evaluation, consider the following true story. An unsaved boy, although invited often to church, was never open to attending, but when asked to go to camp with a friend, he willingly came to camp. During the week, he accepted Christ as his Savior. Before he left camp, arrangements were made to take him to church the very next Sunday, and he was eager to go. Using the camping ministry tool made a difference and was worth the investment!

When you look at the value of the camping ministry in reaching young people, strengthening families, and serving churches, think of it as a different ministry tool than you would use at home every week, but yet as an indispensable tool to furthering the cause of Christ and the mission of both the family and the church. Consider the specialty aspects of this valuable ministry tool—ready to do ministry in a unique way.

A Proven Tool

Why has camp become one of the most effective tools for churches and families to use in fulfilling their biblical responsibilities? Churches use camp to fulfill their Great Commission responsibilities in reaching and making disciples. Families use camp to fulfill their biblical responsibilities to "bring them [their children] up in the nurture and admonition of the Lord" *(Ephesians 6:4)*. Both are obligated to follow the example of Christ's upbringing by helping youth "[increase] in wisdom and stature, and in favor with God and man" *(Luke 2:52)*.

For generations, young people have made life-changing, spiritual decisions at camp—decisions some resisted for years. Dr. Walter Fremont, former Bob Jones University Dean of the School of Education and an extraordinary teacher of the youth ministry classes, surveyed the incoming freshman classes. His survey averages showed 30% were saved at a summer youth camp, and another 30% dedicated their lives to the Lord at a summer camp or youth retreat (*Forming a New Generation*, page 93). A high percentage of pastors and missionaries today made milestone decisions at camp. When I preach in many churches across the nation, I am amazed at the numerous times pastors lean over before the message to tell me about turning-point decisions for salvation, dedication,

> " Being at camp brought me closer to God, closer to my church family, and most importantly, brought my sister and I closer. We are trying to heal as a family and I believe this retreat has helped us do that.

or restored relationships with the Lord they made at camp as children or teens.

Camp done correctly is an effective tool for presenting the gospel and challenging young people and adults with God's Word. In *Colossians 1:28–29*, the Apostle Paul speaks of presenting every man perfect in Christ Jesus:

> *Whom we preach, warning every man, and teaching every man in all wisdom; that we may present every man perfect in Christ Jesus: Whereunto I also labor, striving according to his working, which worketh in me mightily.*

The camp ministry is a tool, an effective and in-all-wisdom methodology, for preaching and teaching to bring others to Christ and to spiritual maturity.

Camp is a harvest-field ministry, because decisions made there are often the culmination of several influences within the body of Christ through the Holy Spirit's work.

> *So then neither is he that planteth any thing, neither he that watereth; but God that giveth the increase. Now he that planteth and he that watereth are one: and every man shall receive his own reward according to his own labor. For we are labourers together with God: ye are God's husbandry, ye are God's building.*
> *1 Corinthians 3:7–9*

Some of the numbers and percentages of young people making decisions at camp may be down today from their historical numbers; but for the most part, it is not because the methodology is any less effective today, but rather because the percentage of young people going to camp is down from what it used to be. Young people today have many voices calling them not only away from the Word, but also away from the places they can hear the Word. The secularization of society identified in the Scriptures as the love of the world is a major enemy of the cause of Christ drawing people away from church, the Christian family, and Christian camps effectively sowing and watering the Word.

A Historical Tool

Christ used a methodology similar to camping when He invited His disciples to retreat into the desert in *Mark 6:31*: "And he said unto them, Come ye yourselves apart into a desert place, and rest a while: for there were many coming and going, and they had no leisure so much as to eat." This change of pace for the disciples was accompanied by the Lord's teaching and the disciples having opportunity for a ministry of service to others.

The beginning of camping as we know it today began in America in colonial times. The first recorded organized camp in the United States was in 1776. Pastor John Waller, a separatist Baptist pastor in Virginia, held the first organized camp meeting. Many camp meetings were held during the 1800s, and the

> " I have learned so much about my relationship with God, my marriage, and forgiveness that I never really realized that it is about. I have also taken things from my past and confessed to the Lord to take and handle them because I can't do it on my own.

origin of the second Great Awakening of the early 1800s is traced to a camp meeting in Kane Ridge, Kentucky, where over 25,000 souls were saved. Camp meetings continued to be more organized, and in the late 1800s, the "Bible Conference Movement" developed at such places as Winona Lake, Indiana. Men like Wilbur Chapman, Homer Rodeheaver, and Billy Sunday ministered to those attending weeks at a time. The brush arbor gave way to open-air tabernacles with sawdust on the dirt floors and preaching going on all day and late into the evenings. Much was accomplished for the Lord in the hearts of the attendees.

What we know today as Christian youth camping began in the early 1900s but expanded rapidly in the late 1940s and 1950s, and many of the largest camps in America trace their roots to that timeframe. Many fundamental Christian camps started in the 1960s and 1970s, with the average start-up date of 1973.

An Indispensable Tool

Without a doubt, organized camping was raised up by the Lord for this time as a service ministry for local churches to reach this generation for Him. The busier today's information-driven lifestyle, the less time people devote to spiritual things; therefore, the more effective the methodology of camp is. A church ignoring Christian camping—or one that does not use it enough—may well be ignoring one of the more effective ministry tools today. Properly using the camping methodology tool facilitates the preaching of the Word of God, allowing it to penetrate the minds and gain the attention of the hearts of campers so they hear and consider the message of the gospel (*2 Timothy 2:7*).

At one time, camp was the premier summer event for church youth groups. However, changes in our society (e.g., easier travel, more entertainment, changing school calendars, and work options) now add other choices besides camp. Also, filling the summer calendar are mission trips, college campus trips, and youth conferences. The average family cannot afford to send their children to every event. The other ministry choices are valuable, but they should not take the place of sending youth to a good camp each summer. Camp is a place where lifetime memories are formed, and life-changing decisions are made.

> *And said, Verily I say unto you, Except ye be converted, and become as little children, ye shall not enter into the kingdom of heaven. Whosoever therefore shall humble himself as this little child, the same is greatest in the kingdom of heaven. Matthew 18:3–4*

BOTTOM LINE

Every occupation has specialty tools called "tools of the trade." Camp ministry is that effective, specialty tool of the trade for pastors, youth pastors, parents, and anyone desiring to reach others for Christ and make disciples. Camp blends adventure, solitude, the presentation of God's truth, and opportunities for decision in a way that is different from everyday ministry in the home or church. Time-tested and well-proven, it is specifically designed to reach people in a busy, what-is-new, what-is-faster society. Options abound for youth and families as they consider how to use both their finances and their time. An understanding of the value of camp will encourage the local church and family to choose this indispensable ministry tool as they endeavor to fulfill their God-given mission.

IS CAMP WORTH IT?

They say a picture is worth a thousand words, but what about three of them? This afternoon I did my rounds of going to different graduation parties from some of our kids here at church. One of the boys was saved two years ago at [camp]. When I was at his home today, he took me to his room and showed me a wall next to his bed. The top picture is a picture of the place where he got saved. The two side pictures are pictures of his cabinmates and his counselor. In the middle is the broken I [brand] which he bought on Saturday after learning what it was all about at the campfire the night before. He told me he is still trying to live a broken life before God. Underneath the broken I is a index card that has his decisions on it from the sponsor reunion. He kept it and keeps it up to remind himself of them.

His week of camp, in his words, "was the most important week in my life." That is why he went to the work of doing all of this on his wall. He's a different boy than he was two years ago. He is a Christian who just finished his senior year in public high school and graduated with a strong testimony in a rough school.

God does amazing work, and I was reminded today of the power of a week of camp.

—Pastor

CHAPTER TWO
The Heart of Camping

In addition to thinking of camp as a tool, we must also recognize it for what it is—simply a method of ministry. Churches have traditionally used a variety of methods to win the lost and disciple believers. Vacation Bible School, Sunday school, area-wide evangelistic meetings, local church revival meetings, and bus ministries are among those different methods. Camp meetings, Bible conferences, retreats, family camps, couples' retreats, youth camps, and pastors' conferences are among the camping methodology used by churches in America both yesterday and today. Understanding what makes this methodology of camp tick by considering this acrostic of the HEART of camping is essential to recognizing the value of camp.

Christian camping is a wise methodology developed for effective, spiritual impact on every camper by the preaching, admonishing, and teaching of Jesus Christ through God's Word, and the work and example of God's servants empowered by the Spirit. This wise methodology has five key ingredients that comprise the HEART of camping:

Hearing the Word of God

Eliminating Worldly Influences and Life's Distractions

Away from Home Overnight in a New Setting

Reflecting on the Word and My Life in a Creation Context

Trained Staff Leading Unique, Organized Activities

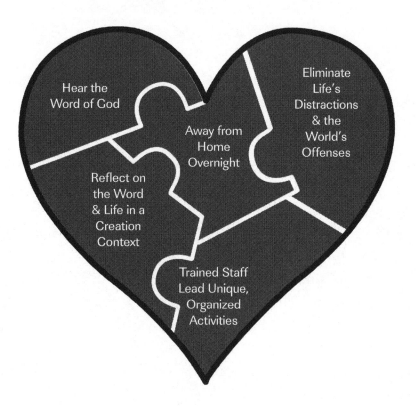

Hearing the Word of God

For the word of God is quick, and powerful, and sharper than any two-edged sword, piercing even to the dividing asunder of soul and spirit, and of the joints and marrow, and is a discerner of the thoughts and intents of the heart. Hebrews 4:12

This verse gives parents two key truths dealing with teaching the Word to young people. The first is to teach diligently, or piercingly, so the Word gets through to their brains. The second is to teach constantly—no matter the situation, in casual and formal teaching—using each teachable moment. An effective camping program applies both principles in designing a week of camp. They figure out how almost every aspect of the campers' experience can be used to diligently point them towards the Lord and the truths of the Word. They look at each aspect of the program to determine how to piercingly deliver truths to the camper through both the formal and informal teaching and preaching times of presenting the Word.

The formal preaching of God's Word in the chapel and evening services should not be minimized just because of many other opportunities used throughout the day to deliver the "spiritual punch" of the Word. The whole day, the entire program and schedule, needs to point toward and support the evening preaching service. The timing of the service needs to be the premier spot in the schedule, coming before the campers are so tired that they cannot concentrate on the preaching of the Word. The service should not be before some big camp event that may cause the young people to forego the invitation time because of what follows. Keeping the spiritual impact as the primary goal helps everyone remember why they are doing camp! Yet it must never be seen as the only platform for spiritual decisions at camp. The Lord did much with one-on-one conversations (camper and cabin counselor) and small groups with His disciples (cabin devotions and discussions), as well as speaking to the multitudes. In all of His teaching, Jesus brought people to a point of decision. He said many times, "He that hath ears to hear, let him hear" (Matthew 11:15). He was really calling for those who had heard His teaching to do something about it!

I thank God I was able to come and listen to His Word! The messages were AMAZING! Every single one spoke to me! I know God had me come for a reason, and I'm so glad I did.

—Father-Son Camper

Eliminating Worldly Influences and Life's Distractions

Believers will never live in a perfect spiritual vacuum—an earthly life without the temptation to sin through the lust of the flesh, the influences of the world, or the attack of Satan. However, Christian camps attempt to lessen the pull of the world. Not all distractions pulling campers away from considering the gospel are sinful, so distraction elimination is two-pronged.

First, eliminate as many offenses as possible—Christ identified them in *Matthew 18:5–10* as stumbling blocks— things that entrap, entice, or cause people to sin. *Hebrews 12:1–2* speaks of laying aside not only sin, but also the weights hindering spiritual life or growth. Therefore, a good camp program identifies and eliminates those hindrances people have back home, allowing the Word to piercingly enter

66It is a great place to be. Very peaceful and isolated enough to get closer to the Lord. The Lord can speak to me without competition with all my business. While I'm here, I'm not Mom, Hun, or "Where's my . . . ?" It is so wonderful to get away from the hustle of everyday life, be with godly people, and renew my walk.

their hearts. Even if some activities are not "sinful," eliminating campers' options for music and entertainment creates a break from the constant noise of the world. The camp environment disrupts normal habits, separates the campers from old friends, disconnects them from their gadgets, and allows them to reach the point where they are ready to listen.

Second, eliminate distractions—such issues as physical and personal needs keeping campers from listening to the preaching of the Word and the Holy Spirit's work. For example, the camp food should be pleasing in taste and quantity. This allows campers to focus on the spiritual message during a service rather than look forward to food at the snack shop or have something to grumble and gripe about. Other areas to scrutinize include cleanliness, cabin comfort, safety, and temperature of meeting rooms. In being concerned about these necessities of life, we follow the lead of our Saviour. On two occasions, He fed the thousands with plenty of leftovers (good food), made the effort to get His disciples away for a rest when they needed it (distractions of daily life), and set up a stage so they heard and saw Him as He taught them (a small boat pushed out from shore). He made sure they heard Him teach and had no grumbling in their stomachs to distract them from hearing what He said.

> *Finally, brethren, pray for us, that the word of the Lord may have free course, and be glorified, even as it is with you.*
> 2 Thessalonians 3:1

Camps typically divide their staff teams into two categories or aspects of the ministry. One is the operations team, and the other is the program team. Both are absolutely essential in the effectiveness of the camping ministry, and nowhere is that more apparent than in this area of eliminating distractions. The operations team needs to view their role as essential for the Word of God to have its maximum effect on the campers throughout their stay at camp. Cleanliness, good food, and safety all play a part in the spiritual results, and a good operations team can make or break a week of camp both from the enjoyment and spiritual aspects. Likewise the program team needs to keep in mind things like scheduling the preaching service in the right time slot and having the campers there on time, alert and ready to hear the Word. Also scheduled in are times of reflection, small group times, and times when counselors can talk to their campers. These times are vital to the success of the camp's spiritual impact aspect. Looking at both these aspects of the camping ministry in a little more depth helps a pastor or youth pastor better understand the utility value of a well-planned program.

Distraction List of the Operations Teams

The operations team has some direct control over the items on its top-ten list. "No answers" may seem like an odd number-one priority, but we have found over the years that the worst thing we

> " I pastor a group of teens here at camp. As I listened to the teens sing last night (Friday) and compared their attitudes and facial expressions to those I saw on Monday and Tuesday, I was so delighted to see how God had used every facet of this wonderful place to work in their lives.

can do when a camper asks a question is to say, "I don't know, and I can't help you find out." A staff member may not know the answer to every question he is asked but should know how to find the answer and be willing to do so.

1. **No answers**—beginning with "When is camp?" and "What does it cost?" all the way to "Where is foosball?" and "Where is my cabin?" When a camper has a question, the answer is the most important thing to them.

2. **No flexibility**—a twenty-four hour schedule demands a bit of flexibility. No flexibility is like saying, "I don't care about you."

3. **Unsafe**—whether real or perceived, if camp is unsafe, campers do not attend.

4. **Electricity**—light, climate control, and curling irons. We have come to a firm reliance on electricity.

5. **Water**—thirst becomes a huge distraction, and the constant provision of water can be taken for granted until it is in short supply.

6. **Housing**—a cabin, a place to lay your head, a place of protection. The first thing campers want to know when they arrive is where they are going to stay for the next few days. A good night's sleep and adequate rest are essential for good attention to the preaching of the Word.

7. **Dirty**—no matter how nice the cabin may be, if it is not clean, it becomes a distraction.

8. **Hot/cold**—whether referring to air, water, or food, people expect these things to be the appropriate temperature.

9. **Horrible food**—since camp spans a number of meals, the more

horrible meals campers endure, the harder it gets for them to be patient, loving, and willing to listen and consider.

10. **Noise/quiet**—few things are worse than the distraction of a weed whacker during the morning chapel invitation. Things become a distraction when quiet is expected, and it turns out to be loud or vice versa.

They have a great staff; the facilities are very clean and beautiful. It was a very easy environment to learn at. I appreciate this week very much. Thank you.

—Counseling Seminar Camper

Distraction List of the Program Team

For the program team, showing no love for campers is the number-one distraction. Exhibiting a selfish or self-centered view is a sure distraction for the camper. An others-first love is an absolute must for ministers (a.k.a. servants) in the camping ministry.

1. **No love**—no love for another means that there is love for just one—a

I realized sometimes it is good both physically and spiritually to have a break from the everyday schedule at home.

34

selfish love. Camp only works with people who choose to love others rather than themselves.

2. **Inconsistency**—our walk and talk should be the same. When they are the same, it is a powerful testimony of God's way working; when they are not, our walk undermines our talk.

3. **Unknown purpose**—why are we doing camp? If a camper thinks camp is only about fun and a time to make friends, he misses what the purpose of camp is.

4. **Unknown needs**—not knowing the needs of your camper produces a one-size-fits-all mentality to camp.

5. **Communication**—talking, listening, and thinking . . . all must happen constantly.

6. **No preparation**—no organization and no planning may work for a few minutes, but it eventually becomes obvious when someone is flying by the seat of his pants.

7. **Staff-centered**—the camper must be the focus and not the relationships or ease of the staff team.

8. **Worldly influence**—the program team must work hard to keep the worldly influence out of its program, including skits, games, and general interaction.

9. **Unmanaged risk**—not everything fun is safe, but the line must be drawn where the balance of risk is firmly on the side of safe.

10. **Never go individual**—a program team that just sees camp only as a crowd misses the opportunity to minister in a personal way.

Away from Home Overnight in a New Setting

Being away from home overnight in a new setting is one of the most important aspects of camp and is often ignored without realizing its value for both adults and youth campers. Although a series of nightly meetings at a church or meetings scheduled at a nearby hotel can be effective, it is not a true camp methodology. By going home every evening, participants do not get away from their familiar settings, and the group going to a hotel discovers a host of distractions to occupy their minds.

Disrupted Comfort Zone and Habits. According to Nielson, the average American television viewer watches 151 hours of television a month—this is an all-time high. Life often becomes a brainless routine. When routines or comfort zones are disrupted, adults and young people are more likely to focus their attentions on their new surroundings, pay closer attention during preaching and teaching times, or spend time immediately after a service thinking about the message and its impact on their lives.

> " It is a peaceful quiet—restores your soul. Wandering in the desert the Lord brought me to His watering hole—and refreshed my soul.

I realize that when I come here, the contrast to living in the city with all the hustle and bustle of life, that I don't spend enough time with [God]. The stillness of the day, the quietness in the air, and beauty that surrounds me causes me to re-dedicate my life to serve the Lord. I want to bottle this feeling and stillness and take it back to the city. Thank you, Lord, for this place and this staff.

Senses on Alert. Campers not only have new surroundings but also are around new people with a new schedule. The new surroundings aspect of Christian camp methodology leaves a lasting, eternal impression. When God's Word is preached or taught, campers are more alert, and their focus can switch to reflecting on the Word as it relates to their lives. When asked, many people fondly remember events at camp as well as key spiritual decisions, while the week before and after disappear in the routine of life.

Reflecting on the Word and My Life in a Creation Context

Often campers come from cities where they are surrounded by paved streets, sidewalks, buildings, power lines, cell towers, bridges, high rises, billboards, and shopping malls. Stars disappear because of all the streetlights, headlights, security floodlights, and brightly lit houses. Camp provides campers a view of creation and an opportunity to get close to it, reminding them the Creator is powerful, interested in them, and loved them enough to die on the cross for them. Having time and opportunity to consider God's Word and their lives in the context of creation is an absolute essential of the camping methodology.

God's creation always points to Him, but the gospel must still be presented. Without a clear gospel presentation, campers may see the Creator but not their Saviour. In the Gospels, 80 percent of Christ's illustrations were from nature. In Psalms, the imagery regarding God, His power, and His majesty comes from descriptions of creation and the laws of nature. Campers are in awe of God when they ponder the vastness of the universe, the power to create from nothing, or the fragile beauty of an intricate wildflower growing only when conditions are ideal. When campers consider the testimony of creation, they have no excuse for not considering God's Word and believing in Him.

> I loved the stars, riding horses, and being away from the everyday of life. I am refreshed through the preaching of God's Word and ready to go back [home] knowing I have a mighty Lord and Saviour!
>
> —Couples' Retreat Camper

When I consider thy heavens, the work of thy fingers, the moon and the stars, which thou hast ordained; What is man, that thou art mindful of him? and the son of man, that thou visitest him? Psalm 8:3–4

"I was blessed by the love of God being present through the staff. Every staff member gave a personal touch that made the camp more memorable.

Know therefore this day, and consider it in thine heart, that the Lord he is God in heaven above, and upon the earth beneath: there is none else. Deuteronomy 4:39

Because that which may be known of God is manifest in them; for God hath showed it unto them. For the invisible things of him from the creation of the world are clearly seen, being understood by the things that are made, even his eternal power and Godhead; so that they are without excuse. Romans 1:19–20

In *Matthew 6:24–30*, God's creation shows He is a loving and providing God. He created and provides for the lilies of the field and challenges believers to have faith in His care for His children. Verse thirty says, "Wherefore, if God so clothe the grass of the field, which today is, and tomorrow is cast into the oven, shall he not much more clothe you, O ye of little faith?"

Throughout the Bible, believers are encouraged to consider God's creation and learn from it. In a creation setting, campers have an opportunity to reflect on what God has already done for them—the sacrifice of Christ upon Calvary. They can also evaluate what changes are needed for them to align with His Word and will.

Go to the ant, thou sluggard; consider her ways, and be wise. Proverbs 6:6

66 I always come away with tools to help me walk closer with the Lord and get convicted of the necessity of filtering all my thoughts and activities through God's Word, not my own preferences.

Only fear the Lord, and serve him in truth with all your heart: for consider how great things he hath done for you. 1 Samuel 12:24

Consider the work of God: for who can make that straight, which he hath made crooked? Ecclesiastes 7:13

I will consider thy testimonies. Psalms 119:95

Now therefore thus saith the Lord of hosts; Consider your ways. Haggai 1:5

For they considered not the miracle of the loaves: for their heart was hardened. Mark 6:52

Looking unto Jesus the author and finisher of our faith; who for the joy that was set before him endured the cross, despising the shame, and is set down at the right hand of the throne of God. For consider him that endured such contradiction of sinners against himself, lest ye be wearied and faint in your minds. Hebrews 12:2–3

Trained Staff Leading Unique, Organized Activities

Designing a program to aid the accomplishment of the camp mission, yet appearing to be simple on the surface, is the result of adjustments and fine tuning. Care must be taken to balance fun activities and the spiritual impact of camp. Using trained staff to lead the games and activities gives the counselors a bridge of relationship when it comes time to discuss spiritual matters, as well as ensuring each activity is balanced in terms of competition, fairness, safety, and fun.

A trained staff team has far-reaching benefits—safety, knowledge of facility and activities available, skill in teaching the various specialized outdoor activities, understanding of the mission, and training in counseling for salvation, full surrender, and consistent Christian living.

Unique, organized activities—games not usually played at home—surprise campers and level the playing field. No young person has an automatic advantage based on prior skills and abilities. In contrast to a public campground where everyone is camping out and doing his own thing in regards to timing, meals, and activities, a camp is organized around its spiritual goals, daily schedule, activities, and meals. Staff plan, organize, lead, and control activities specific to the age group's skill level, fun quotient, and interest level. The schedule balances activity and rest to help campers stay awake when God's Word is preached. Each day includes small group discussions, one-on-one talks, teachable moments, personal devotions, and preaching and teaching of God's Word. Not only is the schedule planned, but so is the environment. This importance can be underscored when attempting a spiritual retreat with a youth group in a public campground while competing with distractions of loud music or motorcycles.

In planning the schedule, many areas are considered: nutrition, sleep, safety, excitement, new experience opportunities, adventure, quiet personal time, contemplation, individual youth group needs and goals, new friendships forming, and the overall purpose of reaching young people for the Lord Jesus Christ, strengthening families, and serving churches. Activities must stay in balance with spiritual objectives. Camp leadership must always remember to keep program activities in balance with the spiritual impact goals and never allow activities to become so important, tiring, or exciting that they diminish or detract from the spiritual goals.

What Is the Heart of Camping? Camp is a Place of Decision.

As we consider all aspects of the HEART of camping, we must remember that it is still the campers' responsibility to make their own decisions as the Word of God is sown and watered in their hearts (see appendix D). They either respond by receiving it as it is in truth, the Word of God, or some may say, "We will hear thee again of this matter" (*Acts 17:32*). It is always heart-breaking to see some campers say no to the convicting power of God. When some reject the gospel, we must remember the effectiveness of camp: extended time away from home and elimination of many distractions from hearing the Word of God, all the while being drawn by the Holy Spirit. Camp is one of the very few settings where that kind of repeatability and extended invitation is a given or is even possible. What happens at camp while campers are considering the Word? The camping methodology is really not complicated. We can boil it down to five simple things campers do while at camp:

1. Meet—preaching and teaching times

2. Eat—food service, three times a day, plus snacks

3. **Sleep**—cabin time including sleep

4. **Play**—activities and fun times

5. **Consider**—reflect on the Word, the message of creation, and example of others in relation to personal life issues

These five things happen at every camp. How much they happen and how effective they are depends upon the camp's philosophy of ministry. The staff spends a majority of their time working on these five things in order to make camps comfortable and enjoyable. The program team is responsible for both **meet** and **play**, organizing the schedule around meeting times when a speaker shares the Word of God; playing is interspersed throughout the schedule with activities and game times. The operation team is responsible to make sleep and eat times enjoyable experiences.

Of the five things, the one responsibility of the camper is to consider—to listen to the Word of God and take the time and effort to ask, "What needs to change in my life in order to conform to God's Word?" The work of considering can be uncomfortable and difficult. A camper is faced with truth of his not meeting up to God's standard. He has no excuses and must make a choice for change. Camp staff and church leaders cannot make the decision. It is the camper's responsibility to consider his own life. However, the program team can facilitate this aspect by programming time into the schedule to allow for this, and the operation team can facilitate this by having benches and spots strategically placed around camp where such moments of contemplation can take place.

Ponder the path of thy feet, and let all thy ways be established.
Proverbs 4:26

Life at home is often so busy and full, not allowing time for freedom from distractions to really consider and ponder their ways. Interruptions and everyday stresses fill each waking moment. Camp becomes the once or twice a year opportunity to consider the adjustments necessary to become more Christ-like. A decision is the fruit of time well spent when young people and adults consider their lives in the context of creation and in light of the truth of the Word.

BOTTOM LINE

Camp is a method of ministry with five key ingredients:

- **H**earing the Word of God

- **E**liminating Worldly Influences and Life's Distraction

- **A**way from Home Overnight in a New Setting

- **R**eflecting on the Word and My Life in a Creation Context

- **T**rained Staff Leading Unique, Organized Activities

Meshing with the five things campers do each day: meet, eat, sleep, play, and consider.

Camp's worth is substantiated when people consider the HEART of camping and the five things campers do at camp, and how they all work together to make **camp a place of decision.**

IS CAMP WORTH IT?

Jill [name changed] was having a rough week. We were making great progress by Wednesday afternoon; she was opening up during our one-on-one, and even laughing some. Then on Thursday we went canoeing. She didn't want to get wet, so I put her in a boat with one other girl that didn't want to get wet. Through different circumstances, her boat ended up tipping over, and she thought she was drowning. She was, however, able to stand; she just didn't realize it. I gave her a walking assist to the dock. She got out and ran away from me. For the next hour, she would not even look at me. I sat there with her while she was crying, and just prayed. I knew that for a homesick girl, being this scared and away from mom was going to be rough. I was talking to her about fear and never being alone, reminding her that God is always with her. She was definitely not in her comfort zone. But God worked in her heart. She came to realize that she was safe and that she was never in any danger. For the rest of the week, Jill was a different girl. She opened up to the camping experience. She was willing to be comfortable with her new cabinmates and me as her counselor. I truly believe that this was her turning point. Being away from home, for a week, in a new setting, out of her comfort zone, allowed for a heart change in this ten-year old girl. Jill's story is always in my head. I'm thankful for a place for kids to come, to get away just for a few days, and learn that different surroundings are ok!

Her comment to me, "Miss Aricka, thanks for saving my life and reminding me that God is always with me, even way out here!"

CHAPTER THREE
How Is Value Determined?

Is value based solely on the cost of something? Let me answer this with an illustration of the "hot dog saw." Few people outside the world of avid woodworking hobbyists or professional woodworkers ever heard of such a saw. When I first heard of it, I asked myself, "Who wants or even needs a saw designed to cut hot dogs in two?" Needless to say, I missed the point of the message, for the claim to fame of the hot dog saw is not what it can do (cut hot dogs), but what it cannot do (cut hot dogs). This powerful five horsepower table saw cannot cut through a hot dog. As a matter of fact, when running at 3750 rpms, it barely nicks a hot dog before the blade stops dead in its tracks. This new saw is a revolutionary tool putting the safety of the woodworker first on its priority list by not amputating a finger if a mistake is made. Having experienced such a near miss personally, I decided to pay close attention to the demonstration. I was amazed to see it in action but surprised it costs twice as much as other top quality saws, and three times more than some economy models. I walked away shaking my head, thinking it was not worth the cost. Later, in another store I was told that even though these saws are

This week at camp was one of the best weeks of my life. I learned a lot of how God is and how much He loves us. I made a decision to make my life count and to give more glory to God. I am so thankful that the Lord allowed me to come this year!

more expensive than other models, the store sold more of them than the other three biggest brands all put together. The determination of an item's value is not always based on cost, but upon other factors as well.

Church leaders must be careful to address the real and differing costs involved in camp ministry, which is always more than just the monetary expenditures: time spent making all the arrangements to go to camp, including registration details with the camp, the promotion and sign-ups, travel arrangements and costs, cost of time organizing the trip within the context of a busy ministry, and the actual camp fee tacked on to all the other costs. Many currently wrestle with the value of camp due to their limited budgets. The Lord has helped us evaluate our decision by His principle of **"one is worth more than all"** in *Matthew 16:26*, "For what is a man profited, if he shall gain the whole world, and lose his own soul?"

How do we answer, "Is it worth it?" This is a quandary we all wrestle with as we make choices spending our precious few resources. Parents go through mental exercises each year, deciding if sufficient funds are available to send their children to camp again that year. That struggle does not stop in the home but also affects church leaders and youth workers as they look at their scarce resources. The answers for some are easy; past experiences convince them that regardless of the cost, time, and effort, camp is a tool to continue using. Others with different experiences or no experience at all with the camping methodology struggle with the decision.

As we look at the questions and find the answers surrounding the issue of a camp's value, we must not fall into the trap of thinking we are living under different circumstances than those before us. The trials and tribulations we face today have been common to man since the days of Noah. When Noah was asked to quit what he was doing for a living and build a boat, God used Noah's obedience and saved his family, by faith, in the midst of one of the most wicked cultures this world has ever experienced (*Hebrews 11:7*). I imagine it was much worse than today's society, for certainly more than eight righteous people exist in every one or two billion today (population estimates pre-flood, Rehwinkel, p. 29). We cannot claim exclusive challenges.

As we seek to understand the camp ministry's true value, we must understand a few basics in determining value and worth. This is not a rabbit trail but very important for thinking leaders to grasp. Following are four factors to help determine value and set priorities when expending scarce resources.

Factors Used in Determining Value or Worth

Value is determined by a thorough evaluation of at least four factors meshed together and considered as a whole. Whether or not people want to expend the limited resources they hold in their hands in exchange for the value another holds in his hand is the question. An axiom in the business community says "requests always exceed resources"; if true, this means more options are available than resources to expend for them. Understanding the four factors of value will perhaps help us prioritize the use of our scarce resources.

Intrinsic Factor—considers a product or service's natural or innate merit or value.

If one has a gold ring, it is the value of the gold in the ring. In the case of the hot dog saw, the intrinsic value of one's fingers helped determine its value.

Utility Factor—considers a service or product's effectiveness in producing the desired effects.

Such evaluation compares the promised performance to the delivered outcome. Does it work? Does it do what it says it will do? Does it produce the desired results? If the answers to these questions are negative, then it does not matter how inexpensive the item may be. It is not worth it!

Perception Factor—considers what

This was my first year at camp, and it truly made a big difference in my life. It has been the best experience!

people think and is influenced by advertising and current trends; thus, it is more complex.

For example, a camp having all the cabins with their own internal restrooms is more valuable to Americans today than for past generations. If camp facilities do not keep up with today's perception of normal expectation, they suffer loss of perceived value.

Perceived value is fixed by what people think—their estimation of worth. If a youth group chooses a facility with more rustic facilities, promoting it as a three-star resort is not wise. Rather, challenge the youth to step back in time to a simpler way of life without normal comforts and focus on the real values in life—the eternal values.

Perceived value is sometimes fixed by history, such as an antique or an object owned by an ancestor. Former campers who are now adults often sacrifice to make camp available to their own children. Whatever the cost, it is worth it to have their children experience the same thing they experienced as a child or teen. For those parents, the perceived value is much higher because of their own memories and experiences.

Perceived value is influenced by others. Because of this "value added by perception" factor, it is extremely important to have people give testimonies of camp's impact on them or their children. Likewise, do not overlook establishing perceived value by recommendations and public endorsements by pastors and youth pastors. When I was a youth pastor, my pastor expressed to the congregation the importance of camp for young people and families. His endorsement increased the perceived value of camp and was a key factor in determining whether or not we had an average or excellent registration.

Perceived value changes slowly and is impacted by tradition, technology, and what the camper experiences at home as normal. In the 1930s, my mother went to a camp that had mattresses made of 2x4 frames and three inches of fresh hay to lay your bedroll on. Today our mattresses are much different than in the 1930s. Over the years, what is expected slowly changes. In 1970, a camp was happy to have a phone; in the 1980s, we were wondering if payphones were a good idea; in the 1990s, a couple campers had a cell phone; in 2000s, we got rid of our pay phones, and now we are asked about wi-fi. Perceived value keeps changing with the times.

Market Factor—considers what something can be sold for after factoring in the cost basis.

The bottom line is if something cannot be sold for more than it costs, it soon ceases to exist. This is a measure of the product's efficiency.

Reducing cost by cutting quality or quantity is often what vendors do to handle this issue, and both often undermine true value. Some may use an overseas production facility, even if it comes out as a downgrade in quality. Some may shrink their packages or leave more air space inside the packages. Their motives are usually to keep the bottom line in balance so they can continue to stay in business. This "price/cost squeeze" tries to find a meeting place between what one's cost is and the price someone will willingly pay for the product. If such a balance cannot be achieved, a product ceases to be available. Even classic products around for decades are subject to the market factor of value determination.

For camps or other ministries, this factor boils down to a simple formula: if there is no margin (positive difference between their costs and the prices they charge), there is no ministry. The price they charge plus the donations they receive (cash, goods, and volunteers) must exceed their costs, or the deficit spending sooner or later spells their doom. Finding a balance here is the task of the camp's leadership, but the users of the camp must understand the camp is there for ministry and seldom charges more than absolutely necessary to cover its expenses. Everyone wants more benefits with less cost, but if the camping ministry does not figure out a way to have a positive margin, the camping tool is eventually lost. This fact is true for families, churches, governments, businesses, and also camps.

BOTTOM LINE

The real worth of a product or service is based upon a complex inter-action of all four of these factors:

Intrinsic Factor—a product or service's natural or innate merit or value

Utility Factor—a product or service's effectiveness in producing the desired effects

Perception Factor—what people think which is influenced by advertising and current trends

Market Factor—what something can be sold for after factoring in the cost basis

Churches can use these principles when considering whether a week at camp is worth it. Wise stewardship of a family or church's scarce resources requires an assessment of true value, and assessing true value requires making decisions with eternity in view.

For what is a man profited if he shall gain the whole world, and lose his own soul? Matthew 16:26

IS CAMP WORTH IT?

Max was a fifth grade boy who got saved at camp last summer, but didn't grow much through the year. This year at camp, I had a chance to have a conversation with him about how he needs to start reading God's Word, praying each day and going to church if he is going to grow spiritually. Max made a decision to read his Bible every day. The following is a snippet from our conversation.

Mr. Kris: "So is there a time each day that you could read your Bible, Max?"

Max: "Yeah, midday."

Mr. Kris: "That would be great during the summer, but what about when you go back to school? When could you read your Bible during the school year?"

Max: "Umm . . . midday."

Mr. Kris: "Do you go to a normal school, Max? Do you mean during lunch? I'm not sure I understand."

Max: "It's math class—if you know what I mean." (wink, wink)

As best as I can remember, these are the exact words that Max said in his prayer.

"Hello, God. It's me, Max, again. Well, this time I was hoping that you would help me to remember to read my Bible every day as soon as I get home from school. And even when I'm done with school, help me to still read it every day. (He said a few more words here). Amen."

CHAPTER FOUR

Intrinsic Factor in Determining Value of Camp

Considers a product or service's natural or innate merit or value

The intrinsic value of camp is more than figuring out the value of the food, lodging, or supervising the campers in all their activities and spiritual lessons. Instead of looking at the value of the camp experience, we need to look at the value of the camper who is being served at camp. When considering the value of the camping ministry from that perspective, the intrinsic value of camp begins to take on huge proportions. We look from the vantage point of the primary issues of life—such as the value of life itself, which the Bible defines as "a little time" (*James 4:14*), gone as fast as a vapor rising from a steaming pot.

Consider Shortness of Time

Understanding the value of *life* defined as "time we have upon this earth" is crucial to understanding how valuable camp can be. People have intrinsic value not only because they are created by God and protected by His decrees, but also because He loved them and gave His only begotten Son to die for them as a sinless, substitutionary sacrifice on Calvary's cross. Reaching people for the Lord has intrinsic value since they are eternal and will live somewhere forever, and it is in God's plan to reach them "in time" for the Lord Jesus Christ.

In relation to time, consider two aspects. First, there is a critical time period in every person's life when pride and the hardening of sin is not as big a hurdle to overcome in placing one's faith in the Lord Jesus Christ. In *Matthew 18:3–4*, the Lord identifies this crucial time as our childhood: "Except ye be converted, and become as little children, ye shall not enter into the kingdom of heaven. Whosoever therefore shall humble himself as this little child, the same is greatest in the kingdom of heaven." In Barnes' notes on this passage, he states, "Children are, to a great extent, destitute of ambition, pride, and haughtiness; they are characteristically humble and teachable." When considering this fact, we need to use this short window of opportunity in reaching young people with the gospel. If we think of this as a limited opportunity of seeing young people making life-changing decisions for the Lord, we have a new appreciation of the summer camping methodology.

Consider Need of More Time

Another aspect of time to consider is that some people require more time for understanding to occur and for the Holy Spirit to draw their souls to the

> " I was seriously struggling with depression and being overwhelmed. I was able to get my focus back on God.
>
> —Youth Worker

Lord Jesus, and that extended time is built into a week of camp. A former counselor relates an illustration of this:

> Millie [name changed] did not come with a church group; her foster parents brought her. During the invitation of the salvation message, she went out immediately. As I explained the gospel, she interrupted me constantly with distractions and unrelated questions. As we talked, she asserted she only needed to be saved because she had sinned a few times when she was little—but she did not sin now. She went out after the invitation on Wednesday, and we talked again about salvation and how sin showed itself in our lives. Thursday we talked yet again after the service; although wanting to understand and know she could go to heaven, she still had large gaps in her understanding and did not believe she still sinned. "I'm never even selfish!" she told me, allowing me to describe how selfishness is seen in someone's actions. Throughout the next day, I was able to quietly point out several occasions when she was selfish. As the evening service approached on Friday, many people were praying for her. The invitation came, and again she walked out for counseling. This time, Millie explained much of the gospel to me as I asked her questions. We thoroughly talked through salvation. She finally understood she was a sinner and needed God to wash her sins away if she was to be acceptable to Him. She prayed simply and accepted Christ as her Savior.

Some children hear the gospel in junior church or Sunday school, but they do not make that final decision to call upon the Lord until they are at camp, or vice versa. This shows the importance of the sowing, watering, and reaping principle and our being on the same team together with the Lord in preaching and teaching His Word to not only the lost, but also to those who need to grow in grace as well. At camp, the gospel is given and reinforced all week, giving the necessary time for people to hear the Word, consider it carefully, come to an understanding of the gospel, and respond to the conviction of the Holy Spirit. People need this important time of consideration away from the distractions of life and society.

Consider Differing Needs of People

Camp's intrinsic value must also be viewed from the vantage point of people; after all, the world Jesus died for was not the environment of earth, water, and sky. People are the object of His love, and His sacrificial death on the cross made it possible for them to accept Him as their Savior. Both our young people and adults benefit from camp. Sometimes we concentrate on the youth and forget how much adults also need that time away from the pressures of life to hear the Word preached for several days. The busier our society gets, the time for a distraction-free setting becomes more of a necessity. Gone are the days of two, three, and four-week protracted revival meetings; few churches still schedule week-long meetings. Two or three-day meetings or special emphasis days at church best fit today's busy schedules. This is not an indictment on churches; it is merely a fact of life when the average family has 2½ jobs just to barely exist in today's culture. Remembering people's intrinsic

> I wish that everyone could have the opportunity to come here. I am so blessed to have been able to come again. The Lord blesses this camp more and more each year and touches my heart just the same.

value, pastors can encourage their congregations to set aside some of their limited time and resources to attend a camp retreat to focus on Christ.

Consider Eternity

Finally, no look at camp's intrinsic value can be complete without remembering that the people we are reaching for the Lord are upon the earth for a short time. Living in a temporal and material world, it is easy for us to view time and life as of supreme value, when we should rather focus on eternity. Because our lives are vapors, it is important to take every opportunity to effect eternity in a positive way. One of the intrinsic values of camp is the method's ability to clearly focus people's minds on what is truly important in life and eternity.

A staff member relayed an incident after a mother-daughter retreat. The campers left for home, but one of the cars came back in the front gate about a half hour later. A camper got out of the car crying but told our staff member not to worry. She said after listening to the messages all week, she thought she might not be saved. She expressed this to her mother on the way home; they stopped the car while on the camp road, and her mother led her to the Lord. They drove back to camp to share her story and testimony with the staff team and to write her decision in our "Book of Decisions." This is a perfect example of the time it takes for some sowing the seed, some watering, but God giving the increase.

Consider What God Values

Let us never forget that in ministry we are working with the most valuable thing in the world, an eternal soul made valuable by the "unspeakable gift of God" (*2 Corinthians 9:15*).

> *Again, the kingdom of heaven is like unto treasure hid in a field; the which when a man hath found, he hideth, and for joy thereof goeth and selleth all that he hath, and buyeth that field. Again,*

*the kingdom of heaven is like unto
a merchant man, seeking goodly
pearls: Who, when he had found
one pearl of great price, went and
sold all that he had, and bought it.
Matthew 13:44–46*

Such stories help us focus on the value
of not wasting any time in reaching our
precious children for the Lord. This
also brings to mind an incident that
happened while at a Christian college recruiting summer staff for counseling positions. I had the privilege of
teaching the camping ministry's value
to local churches to the preacher boys
class. At the end of the class, a young
man came up to me and said, "I am here
today studying for the ministry because
of a decision I made at your camp in the
fourth grade." He went on to recount
that while he was at camp he dedicated
his life to the Lord and surrendered
to be a pastor one day. When he went
home after camp, his parents told him
they were moving to the other side of
the country because of his father's job,
and he did not have the opportunity
to attend our camp again. What an
encouragement to hear his testimony
of God using our camp ministry ten
years earlier to show him His will for
his life. Yes, it is worth it all! It is worth
it because some decisions made mean
a soul will be in eternity with the Lord,

66 The peaceful
nature around us
cleared our minds. It
was wonderful. The love
of Jesus was in every
nook and cranny.

64

and other decisions made by children, young people, and adults result in a changed life—and sometimes a lifetime of service for our Savior. **The camping methodology has intrinsic worth because, in time, we accomplish that which lasts for eternity!**

BOTTOM LINE

To better understand the true value of camp, we need to consider the value of the camper being served, not just the physical aspects of camp. In doing so, we will soon see the eternal value of camp. Considering time, people, and eternity will help us see the bigger picture of camp's intrinsic value.

Time. Each person has a window of time in their life when the effects of pride and sin's hardening are not as great an impediment to placing their faith in Christ. Childhood is a limited opportunity to reach young people with the gospel. Camp is designed around this critical time. A week of camp is also designed to give additional time needed for each camper to hear the Word, consider it carefully, and respond to the Holy Spirit's conviction.

People. As God's special creation and objects of His great love, people have a God-given eternal value. Christ died for the souls of people. And God desires each eternal soul to fully know Him. Camp is valuable because it can impact the eternal destiny of each person with the knowledge of who God is.

Eternity. Life is a vapor. The value of this life is found in preparing the soul for eternity. Camp's worth is found in its eternal perspective. Camp is used to focus people's minds on what is truly important in life and eternity.

IS CAMP WORTH IT?

Prayer Chapel journal entries

Thanks for having me come to this camp. I am glad I came because I have learned more about You.

Many people probably wonder why there would be a camp out in the middle of nowhere in the desert. As I have been here, I've realized that this isn't a desert at all. Lord, your living water is constantly being showered on this camp.

Thank you for bringing me to camp to teach me what brokenness really is. It is more than knowing You with my mind. It is knowing You with my heart fully surrendered to you so that I would die daily to my own selfish way and live completely for you, God.

God is here. Your kindness brings tears to my eyes and refreshment to my soul.

CHAPTER FIVE

Utility Factor in Determining Value of Camp

A product or service's effectiveness in producing the desired effects

Effectiveness is often measured by numbers, and certainly, if we only look at the number of salvation and other decisions for the Lord, the camping ministry holds its own in that regard. But the effectiveness of camp is not measured by numbers alone. We do the Lord and Holy Spirit an injustice if all we do is compare ourselves in a quantity- based manner. For that reason, we do not list numbers and statistics in this little volume. It is sufficient to say the Lord uses the camping ministry to reach people for Him who may not be reached any other way.

Domino Effect

We see the domino effect in action in the lives of campers and staff. After attending camp, campers share with others at home the life-changing message of the Word of God they experienced. For instance, two cousins attended camp, got saved, and shared their testimonies back home. As a result, the church leadership was able to lead nine other family members to the Lord, including both pairs of parents. Eight were baptized and joined the church. The pastor and church family were overwhelmed with joy and wrote us a letter with the testimony of God's working in lives. Another example of this is what God is doing in the lives of the summer staff counselors and volunteers. Undoubtedly, the spiritual by-product from these servants of the Lord making life-changing decisions for the Lord is huge. We call such results the domino effect of camp decisions.

Last summer a boy (I think his name was Chase) came to camp and got saved. The testimony of his sponsors was that his life truly changed—he was a new creation in Christ, and it showed. This summer Chase came back and brought along his older brother Tyler. On the first night, after hearing his fellow-campers giving their testimonies, Tyler asked his counselor what it meant to be saved. The next day, Tyler got saved. Tyler made at least one decision every night of the week. He also got up early on a couple of the mornings and read his Bible of his own accord. He asked very good questions all week long. He was truly a joy to watch, and it started the year before when his younger brother got saved.

> " When I left camp last Saturday morning, I felt refreshed, spiritually encouraged, and itching to get back home and serve the Lord with more passion.
>
> —Pastor

Unintended Consequences

Unintended consequences are not planned, but we often hear of them happening as a result of decisions made at camp. I met a father whose son was applying to counsel for a summer at Ironwood. The father told me the summer he spent at our camp over twenty years earlier was "the spiritual pivoting point" of his life. In another incident, I spoke to a pastor on the east coast who counseled here a summer, and he said it was the "most phenomenal summer of his life." We may not go into the summer camp season intending to witness such long-lasting spiritual effects on our summer staff, but God has innumerable ways of using the camp ministry. One evidence of the spiritual growth and value of serving on summer staff is the high percentage of summer staff who are the children of pastors and those in ministry. These leaders recognize the value and encourage their children to consider a summer or two of ministry at camp.

> Looking back at the ladies' retreat, the faces of many ladies carrying burdens and heartaches come to mind. There was a broken-hearted lady whose husband had committed suicide just a few short weeks before camp. It was such a privilege to love her and the friend that she came with as they began to work through the ripple effect of this tragedy. How amazing to realize that our speaker for that retreat, chosen several years ahead of the date, was uniquely prepared of God to meet the specific needs of this precious lady and that the steps of each person was ordered by Him to meet in this place at this time.
>
> —Women's Retreat camper

Harvest Time

These examples of "camp works" stories are encouraging to remember, and I have kept a file through the years of such testimonies. They are a reminder that **camp is worth it**—that harvest time does come. Scripture frequently uses farming metaphors—plowing, sowing, cultivating, pruning, fertilizing, and reaping—to depict the application of God's truths in our lives.

> *So then neither is he that planteth any thing, neither he that watereth; but God that giveth the increase. 1 Corinthians 3:7*

> *For he that soweth to his flesh shall of the flesh reap corruption; but he that soweth to the Spirit shall of the Spirit reap life everlasting. And let us not be weary in well doing: for in due season we shall reap, if we faint not. Galatians 6:8–9*

> *Say not ye, There are yet four months, and then cometh harvest? behold, I say unto you, Lift up your eyes, and look on the fields; for they are white already to harvest. John 4:35*

Getting young people and adults to stop, slow down, and listen to God's Word is harder and harder in today's hurry-up interruption-filled society. With a well-planned camp schedule, campers have an easier time focusing on God's Word. The seed of God's Word is often sown and watered at home or in the local church. As a result, camp is often a harvest time for decisions.

"A man who went to our couples' retreat prayed to receive Christ this past Sunday. He said he had watched people at the retreat and at other things at church, and he saw a difference in their lives that he wanted. Thank you for your faithful service to us and our people every year when we come to retreat!

And the Spirit and the bride say, Come. And let him that heareth say, Come. And let him that is athirst come. And whosoever will, let him take the water of life freely. Revelation 22:17

God Gives the Increase

The law of the harvest is that if one sows and another waters the seed of God's Word, then God sees their efforts as one and gives the increase of a harvest—often at camp— in the form of decisions made for Him. This is not a matter of arm twisting or manipulation, but simply doing what Jesus did over and over in the Scriptures. In His teaching, He brought people to points of decision and left it to them to choose. But we must never forget the law of the harvest: if we sow and water, then God gives the increase! (*1 Corinthians 3:7*)

One long-term camp staff worker said, "I never get tired of seeing God give the increase as we see so many decisions for Him each summer." As a youth leader was walking through the camp dining room recently, I said something like, "Still hanging in there, huh?" His answer took me by surprise. He said, "I sure am. I have been bringing juniors to camp here and preaching to them for twenty-one years now! This might be the last year for me, but I said that last year, and the year before too—I just love preaching to these young people; they just soak it up every year." This youth pastor knows the value of camp in reaching his young people for the Lord!

Taking the Next Spiritual Step

We train our summer staff to discover where their campers are spiritually and how to lead them to the next spiritual step. Asking a few questions and listening to the answers with discerning ears seems easy. The need may be clear, but knowing the next step of growth is often more challenging. Keeping four simple decision principles in mind helps counselors identify their campers' next spiritual steps.

1. **Decide to accept and identify with the Lord Jesus Christ as God.**

This is the step of salvation, assurance of salvation, publicly identifying with the Lord by a testimony of their salvation at camp, and a decision to discuss baptism with their pastors as they return home. Each summer, we see 60–80 percent of the unsaved young people coming to camp accept the Lord as their Savior.

Sadly, this number is not as big as it used to be because fewer unsaved children come to camp. Many unsaved children and teens from unchurched families do not see the value in going to such a church camp. If someone invites these young people to camp or provides a scholarship for them to attend camp, they often willingly go. The use of such funds in camp ministry can be traced to a healthy portion of the salvation decisions made each summer at camp.

2. **Commit to a lifelong process of fellowshipping with God.**

This is a decision to be faithful in daily devotions of prayer, Bible reading, and confession of sin. It may seem like a simple decision, but next to salvation, it can have the greatest long-term result in those making the decision.

" I grew closer to the Lord and found the next step to take in my walk that has been eluding me for some time.

3. **Present one's life to God with the goal of pleasing Him.**

This is a decision of full surrender to the Lord and a willingness to do whatever the Lord wants in life by seeking, yielding, and following His will. *Romans 12:1*

This is a decision of full-time service for some, and it is important to give our young campers the opportunity to respond positively to such a call from God and make it public at camp.

4. **Transform progressively by yielding to God's will.**

This is a series of decisions for living a consistent Christian life through campers allowing the authority of God's Word and the conviction of the Holy Spirit to work in their hearts, influencing them to yield to God and make the life-changing decisions necessary to grow in grace and become spiritually mature and thoroughly furnished to do God's will. *Romans 12:2; 2 Timothy 3:16–17; 2 Corinthians 3:18; 2 Peter 3:18*

Holy Spirit at Work

We may all be a bit guilty of going to extremes; we either have too much emotion and persuasion or too little when it comes to presenting the gospel to our young people. According to *2 Corinthians 5:11*, the Scripture is quite clear about persuasion being part of man's duty as he shares the Word with others.

Knowing therefore the terror [fear] of the Lord, we persuade men; but we are made manifest unto God; and I trust also are made manifest in your consciences.

However, we must always remember it is the Holy Spirit's work in drawing hearts to Christ and do all we can to facilitate His work. This involves eliminating distractions cluttering a camper's attention during a service, at times of teaching, or even at a time of personal reflection. Certain aspects of entertainment, music, and culture quench the Holy Spirit. *1 Thessalonians 5:19* tells us to make sure we do not quench the Holy Spirit. *Quench* used here means to pour water on a fire so as to douse it or extinguish it. In some way or another, the Holy Spirit can be quenched, and His influence in drawing campers closer to the Lord can be diminished. The options a young person has back home to divert his heart from the conviction of the Spirit are numerous indeed—e.g., music, television, social media, video games, internet, dvd's, telephone, texting. While at camp for a week, those options are considerably diminished. A purposeful schedule and program at camp can effectively facilitate an atmosphere that is beneficial for a harvest of decisions for Christ as the Holy Spirit works.

BOTTOM LINE

The effectiveness of camp in not measured simply by numbers of decisions made for Christ. The Holy Spirit uses His Word at camp on a much greater scale than what we can see simply on a quantity-based evaluation. Additional evidences showing camp's value is the domino effect, or campers sharing with others the life-changing message of God's Word they experienced at camp. Camp's ministry also reaches into the lives of the summer counselors and staff as they are exposed to the same powerful Word of God and are changed to be more Christ-like as they allow the Holy Spirit to work in their hearts during a summer of service. Unintended consequences of the camp ministry are also a measure of camp's value. One soul touched long ago, maybe just once, maybe indirectly, attests to camp's far-reaching worth.

Camp's impact can also be viewed through the "law of the harvest" perspective. Seeds of God's Word can be sown and watered at home, at church, or in camp services and counseling times, and the camper often comes to a point of decision at camp. Trained staff are on the lookout for each camper's spiritual needs and are equipped with the tools to lead them to the next step of spiritual growth through the decisions they make. Four simple decision principles are used to identify a camper's next spiritual step.

Camp is in the business of facilitating God's work in hearts by eliminating or reducing the distractions that quench the Spirit and by quieting the surroundings of each camper so he or she can be drawn by the Holy Spirit to the next step of spiritual growth.

IS CAMP WORTH IT?

Hello , Mr. Kris. I am _____'s mom. He met you at camp a few weeks ago. I just wanted to tell you what a HUGE difference you have made in my son's life. He has done a complete about face on all of his negative behaviors. He is faithfully reading his Bible each night. We have started spending that time together as he needed some help understanding what certain words meant, but it has turned into some highly valuable mother-son time. To be honest, when he came home he asked to go with me to my home group which I, of course, said, "I don't know. Can you behave this time?" He turned to me and flat out said, "Mom, I am saved now, and I am done with that behavior. I want what Mr. Kris has. You don't need to worry about me anymore." To put it mildly, I was stunned. He has been in a Christian school since he was two, but no one had managed to reach him like you did. I truly believe the Holy Spirit was working hard that week. I hope you will be at camp next year. My son will definitely be back. Thank you for your ministry.

—E-mail to camp speaker

CHAPTER SIX

Perception Factor in Determining Value of Camp

Considers what people think and is influenced by advertising and current trends; thus, it is more complex.

Many Christians bristle, and rightly so, at the gimmicks used in previous generations to get more numbers in Sunday school than they had the previous year at the same time. Such excessive gimmicks along with materialistic motivations and pragmatic manipulations of people to perform without the power of the Holy Spirit created hollow victories. Such excesses caused many ministries to pull back sharply on their efforts to promote upcoming events in their church, while others found a balance, not wanting to throw the baby out with the bath water. So wherever a church finds itself in regards to advertising, American commerce says loudly and clearly, "It works!" By good advertising, products sell, politicians are elected, and propositions for the ballot rise or fall, but we ask if there is a place for it in our endeavors to advance the cause of Christ.

Are Recommendations (or Promotions) Biblical?

Ministries must be careful to not substitute slick advertising for the power of the Holy Spirit or manipulation for the true motivation of responding to God's directing when presented with a need (*Romans*

12:1). Such carefulness must also be discerning in not eliminating a tool the Lord allows us to use in advancing His cause upon the earth. Good examples of recommendations are given numerous times in the book of Acts: one believer urged a local assembly to trust another believer (Barnabas recommending Saul); the church in Jerusalem endorsed Paul's gospel message (letter to new believers in Antioch and Galatia from the Jerusalem church in *Acts 15*); believers in Ephesus sent a recommendation letter with Apollos to the believers in Corinth so they would receive him with open arms and ears (*Acts 18:27*). Because of the numerous times we find such verbal and written recommendations from one believer to others, we must conclude this is one of the ways God chooses to encourage others while still maintaining purity in His church.

Recommendations and promotions from youth leaders, parents, and church members blessed by a retreat are effective. Pastors have the opportunity of helping further the cause of Christ by their words and enthusiasm for what they found helpful to them and to their families. When someone is vacillating on whether or not to send his children to camp or go to an adult retreat himself, a word of recommendation, privately or

> " We're really excited to see where my dad went to camp as a kid. We heard your camp is amazing, and we look forward to learning more about God this summer.

82

publicly, often impacts the choice. Why does one recommend camp to another? Because he personally knows by observation or participation the effectiveness of a camp ministry, the trustworthiness of the message preached there, and the care for the campers.

Which Recommendations Are Most Helpful?

Recommendations based on what people think are far less valuable than recommendations based on what they know. For that reason, it is helpful for church leaders to participate or observe the retreats offered at their local camp. Additionally, just because they know the value does not mean they automatically share that with others, and this comes back to the reluctance some leaders have (perhaps because of reasons already addressed above) to encourage others to use the camp ministry as a tool. Camp is an effective tool for the family and church, and those knowing its value can further the cause of Christ by sharing that information with others.

What about the Recommendation Content?

So what should be dealt with in this matter of the perception factor? Leaders need to consider both the negative and the positive in determining the content of their recommendations. Some of the negatives needing to be addressed occasionally are some of the negative stereotypes associated with camps today: camp food, poor supervision, never-ending sermons or invitations, and uncomfortable cabins. Many camps have diligently addressed these issues in recent years and do not deserve such negative stereotypes, so leaders experiencing such improvements personally can help set the record straight. If one such area is still lacking, they can put the best possible light on it for those participating and know the overall experience is a plus for the Lord and the camper. If leaders find themselves unable to honestly and wholeheartedly recommend the camp they are using, they owe it to that camp, as well as their own church congregation, to go to the camp's leadership personally and address the issues. Such meetings are almost always productive, appreciated, and an aid to improvement.

Perceived value is a potentially powerful inducement to determine value and can be greatly influenced by advertising media, promotions at church, or the recommendations of others. Such was the case for me when I considered purchasing the hot dog saw. In the span of a few months, I chanced upon two friends involved in woodworking. One enthusiastically told me a personal account of the saw saving his index finger and a good portion of his hand. After that conversation, I went to the store and looked again at those saws with a new perspective. Later I talked with another friend who lost a fingertip the hot dog saw would have saved had he been using one. Both testimonies, one positive (it worked) and one negative (I should have used it), helped me immensely when it came to making my final decision. In the same way, testimonies of camp experience given at church help others determine the value of camp.

Are Perceived Goals Being Met?

Fun

Church leaders can focus on the three goals of a good camp. The first goal of fun and adventure is not only for the

> 6 6 Your mission statement is truly lived out. Christ's love shines through all your staff. Not only would I come back, I am going to report to our youth leaders and encourage them to bring the youth to camp.

children but also for the leadership. They know it is easier to get young people signed up for camp if their past experiences have been positive. We find it interesting that when asked about a week of camp, many young people focus more on the impact their counselor had upon them rather than upon the fun, adventure, and activities. But the goal of fun is the focus of our presentations to the young people in a church, and it definitely encourages them to go.

Safety

The second goal is for the parents, and it deals with safety and care. Parents want to know their children are well cared for in body as well as in spirit. They are concerned about health issues, food, security, supervision, associations, and safety being factored into all activities their children enjoy. Parents know children do dumb things if left to themselves and what little pressure it takes to influence them into unsafe territory. They want to know about the ministry's maturity and reputation in providing a trained staff who are mature enough to say no when necessary or modify activities to minimized areas of exposure. Leadership must settle the anxieties of parents trusting their children in the hands of someone else. If church leadership does not address this issue each year (even if no one is asking the questions about safety), they will find it more difficult to generate enthusiasm among the parents. The perception of parents about the safety and security of their children greatly impacts whether they believe camp is worth it or not.

Spiritual Impact

The final goal deals with the goals of the church and the parents— the spiritual impact a week of camp or a retreat will have upon the campers. If you are going to the right kind of camp, it cannot exist without this goal being constantly satisfied. It is important for pastors, youth pastors, and parents to share the spiritual goals and recount past life-changing decisions with the congregation in order to keep the enthusiasm for spending their limited resources for this endeavor. A good camp has fun and adventure, safety and care, and makes a spiritual impact on campers' lives.

One group that comes here year after year for couples' retreats almost always introduces us to a couple who came the previous year, already planning to separate if things did not change in their marriage. In coming to a retreat, they made a decision to line up their lives and marriage with the teachings of the Word, and in doing so, are not only still together a year later but thriving in that marriage. The numbers of couples in that church who have had their whole lives and families impacted spiritually in a major way is a constant recommendation to those in the church wondering if it is worth the time, money, and hassle to come with their church to a couples' retreat several hours from their home. The testimonies surrounding them keep saying, we cannot afford **not to go**!

A number of years ago, I delivered a commencement address at a Christian school graduation with fourteen graduating seniors. During the ceremony, testimonies were given, focusing on their years in school and its impact upon them. This school has traditionally selected three different retreats at our camp for their pupils to attend: one in the fourth grade, one in the middle school years, and one specifically designed for high

> 66 Many years ago I sent my kids to camp, not even realizing the sanctuary it would one day become for me. Now, as a mom of adult children, I take refuge in the quietness of your hand and heart. A mom's heart is often a fearful and burdened place.
>
> —Prayer Chapel journal

school leadership. Eleven of the fourteen referenced the impact one of those retreats had upon them during their years in that school. Such testimonies go a long way in understanding the spiritual impact of camp and in establishing the mental attitude of value by the people in the congregation. Testimonies given in church on Sunday night or in prayer meeting after the youth or adults return from a camp or retreat are one of the best things a church leader can do in establishing the true value in going to camp again the next year.

To properly address the perception factor value of camp, real effort must be made. This effort to influence others' perception is best done by leaders who have experienced the value of camp personally through either participation or by observation of the spiritual impact upon others. Once understood, they can address and answer questions regarding the intrinsic and utility values of this effective tool to reach today's encumbered society.

BOTTOM LINE

Camp's value is affected by how it is perceived. A key method in shaping the way a camp is perceived is the tool of recommendation. As the blessings of God's work in individual hearts are passed on through recommendations to others, people can more accurately determine the value of that camp ministry. These promotions can take the form of a testimony by a pastor or leader about a camp's effectiveness or the personal testimony of an individual camper about the Lord's work in his or her heart. These testimonies, or "promotions," are powerful and effective. Although we must be careful not to turn camp promotion into slick advertising, we should also not eliminate the tool of recommending a ministry for its effectiveness in people's lives.

It takes work to properly address the perception value of camp. Leaders can focus on the three goals of a camp which are key ingredients of perception: fun, safety, and spiritual impact. The most equipped leaders to do this job are ones who have personally experienced the value of camp's impact on lives. These are the leaders who, after accurately promoting a camp ministry, leave their audience with the feeling that they cannot afford to not take part in this effective ministry.

IS CAMP WORTH IT?

One of my favorite campers, a senior in high school from a dysfunctional home, had come to camp because his sister had come to camp the week before. She had received Christ as her Savior, and when she went home she said to him, "You have got to go to this place. They have the answers to everything we've been searching for." I was in the office when they arrived to register him for his week of camp. He was a bit reserved and nervous; she was beaming. He was full of questions; he came wanting answers. I think he was saved before the end of the first day. That was two years ago. This summer he came back. He had gone home and slowly had slipped back into the drugs and immorality that was the norm for his friends and family. He told his counselor that he came back to camp because he knew he couldn't live anymore in such misery and unhappiness. He needed to get back the joy of his salvation . . . We prayed for him and watched him struggle as he really counted the cost and considered the changes that needed to happen in his life. On Thursday he surrendered his life to the Lord. We know that he has gone back to a very tough situation, and we continue to pray that the work that God has begun in his life will be like the seed in the good soil, bearing much fruit.

—Camp staff

CHAPTER SEVEN

Market Factor in Determining Value of Camp

Considers what something can be sold for after factoring in the cost basis

Is Camp Worth the Cost?

When people ask if camp is worth it, they want to hear if the monetary and labor costs are worth sending their children to camp. We could answer by comparing camp to the cost of going to a theme park for several days, paying for lodging and restaurants for the same number of days. We can factor in the savings of not feeding hungry children at home for a week, and financially the answer is a resounding yes! Comparing benefits and the associated costs reveal value. On the other hand, although the question is on monetary value, the true answer is not a monetary answer; how can one put a price on the worth of a soul?

Camp and church leadership sometimes err, though, by trying to spiritualize this very important consideration of everyday life in America. Regardless of our economy's good or bad times, the fact remains that camp costs money and spiritualizing it or glossing over it does not hide that fact. If more goes out than comes in, bankruptcy occurs. This is true for families, churches, businesses, governments, and even camps. Increases in food and energy costs as well as increasing government regulations, fees, and labor laws add to the cost of camp. The pressure camps face in operation costs is huge, and most camps struggle greatly to keep down those costs. They strive to charge as little as possible so more people can use the camp.

On the other side of the coin is the challenge families and churches face with having to deal with the ever-increasing camp cost. This is a real issue to reconcile from both sides. Camps must redouble their efforts to cut costs without cutting the quality necessary to do ministry effectively in today's cultural expectations. Churches can also address this issue by considering the possibility of asking for offerings for camp scholarships, as well as financially helping sponsors to attend camp without losing both a week of work and bearing the cost burden as well. Church leadership can help by putting things into perspective in terms of cost (parents do not have to feed their children at home for a whole week), and by reminding couples what it costs them to go to a secular environment for a retreat for two nights (e.g., lodging, meals, paying for all entertainment or activities).

Parents can understand a camp's value from the perspective of priority. When I

> I appreciate the opportunity to be ministered to in this way—so many great ideas, and so many people who are of like mind concerning the Word of God and its value to young people. I am too complacent and this camp has helped me to see the practical ways to change my focus.
>
> —Youth Worker

served as a youth pastor, parents told me they could not afford to send their young people to camp. When I heard that, I knew it meant one of three things:

1. They truly could not afford it at that time.

2. They did not want to do it, and this was the default excuse they used.

3. They wanted to use the money for something they considered more important; it was a matter of priority for them.

So how does the pastor deal with those issues of market value? First, he can help the needy with scholarship programs, or he can help them raise some of the funds themselves. Many camps have useful ideas in their files for generating the funds to help families with the cost of camp. Secondly, some folks just do not want to go to camp, so they must be dealt with on the perception level of value. Finally, in dealing with priorities, they can remind potential campers how the Lord addressed the priority decisions made between the material and the spiritual.

> *For what is a man profited, if he shall gain the whole world, and lose his own soul? or what shall a man give in exchange for his soul? Matthew 16:26*

> *But seek ye first the kingdom of God, and his righteousness; and all these things shall be added unto you. Matthew 6:33*

Is It Worth the Extra Cost?

As you are contemplating the answer to that question, reflect on the following note from a former summer staff member. He now serves on the staff of a Christian school and church that sends young people to summer camp.

> School has started here, and we're back in full swing. Things are going well. I wanted to let you know about something that

happened at school last week. On Friday, one of our sophomore guys came up to me and asked if we could talk. Being on the lookout for teachable moments, I gladly accepted. He proceeded to tell me about some serious decisions he made at [camp] this summer. This boy comes from a very rough home situation and has taken some huge steps in his Christian walk this year. He told me that he knew it would be tough coming back from camp and facing everything, and he was having a particularly hard time with some anger and bitterness issues toward a family member. I guess things have gotten more difficult for him at home.

Anyway, at one point in the conversation he looked at me and said, "I'm so glad I went to camp this year and got things straightened out. I didn't have anything to live for before, but God has given me a purpose and happiness that I didn't know I could ever have."

I wanted to tell you this story because it encouraged me greatly. It reminded me of how important the camping ministry is . . . and how God is using that ministry. I know that the day-to-day things can cloud the big picture sometimes, but this situation cleared things up for me. I knew it would be an encouragement to you too. Thanks for all that you and [your] staff do.

Is It Worth It . . . with Eternity in View?

The value of camp is most often defined in the mind of the beholder. What is of great value to one person may be seen as something to discard by another person. For the young people going to camp, their value of camp may be different from the ideas of their parents, their church, or the camp staff. However, Scripture lays down a principle for believers to constantly keep in mind: earthly values are temporal and defined by time, and spiritual values are eternally defined.

Matthew 6:33 gives us our priority in life: "But seek ye first the kingdom of God, and His righteousness; and all these things shall be added unto you." *First Timothy 4:8* shows us clearly the relative values of each, "For bodily exercise profiteth little: but godliness is profitable unto all things, having promise of the life that now is, and of that which is to come." *Matthew 16:26* asks a very important question, "For what is a man profited, if he shall gain the whole world, and lose his own soul? or what shall a man give in exchange for his soul?" These questions prompt another question: "What will parents give in exchange for the souls of their children?" *Second Corinthians 4:17–18* sums it up for us: the eternal is more important than the temporal.

> *For our light affliction, which is but for a moment, worketh for us a far more exceeding and eternal weight of glory; While we look not at the things which are seen, but at the things which are not seen: for the things which are seen are temporal; but the things which are not seen are eternal.*

If Christians are going to be in tune with the reality of eternity, they must clearly define their values while living here in time with eternity's values in view.

Although young people in their immaturity may value camp by its fun quotient, and parents are concerned about the cost and safety of camp, viewing camp from an eternal outlook opens up a better perspective and increased value. Local churches would not send their youth to camp, nor would Christian camps be operating, if it were not for the eternal, spiritual impact on campers' lives.

How Can I Determine the Real Value?

The real value of camp then must be defined for its eternal, spiritual benefit. **Value equals benefit divided by cost.** When the goal of camp is the eternal benefit (e.g., decisions made by the campers and the impact of the preaching of the Word on their lives for eternity), and that is divided by the temporal costs (e.g., the price of camp, transportation headaches, time), the quotient is indescribable in value!

$$V = \frac{B}{C}$$

Remember Christ's question, "What shall a man give in exchange for his soul?" The benefit is so great that the cost does not even enter into defining the value. "For God so loved the world that He gave His only begotten Son" (*John 3:16*).

Sometimes we must remember what needs to be done costs more. A biblical example of this truth is the parable the Lord told in *Matthew 18:12–14* about the lost sheep on the mountain.

> *How think ye? if a man have an hundred sheep, and one of them be gone astray, doth he not leave the ninety and nine, and goeth into the mountains, and seeketh that which is gone astray? And if so be that he find it, verily I say unto you, he rejoiceth more of that sheep, than of the ninety and nine which went not astray. Even so it is not the will of your Father which is in heaven, that one of these little ones should perish.*

The shepherd could have justified a good night's sleep in a cozy cottage, but he was willing to pay the extra cost of discomfort, time, and effort to go after the lost sheep. Today's church

66 I did not know many of our ladies personally before this retreat. Now I know how to pray for them and encourage them; and they can better pray for me. We are a family!

uses this biblical principle to rightly justify the cost of missions' programs reaching the lost around the world. Why not also apply that to reaching young people in our own Jerusalem (*Acts 1:8*)? Gone are the days when everyone has a basic understanding and knowledge of the Bible. When we share a Bible at camp with a young person who has never held one, that young person is seldom saved on the first hearing of the gospel. Having a counselor love him, answer his questions, and discuss issues with him, combined with multiple messages from the Word and every aspect of the day pointing to the Lord, means the likelihood of the young person accepting the Lord during that week is over 60 percent.

Camps and churches put forth extra efforts to use the camping methodology. On one hand, churches expend great effort promoting camp, helping with cost (e.g., fund-raisers, scholarships, special offerings), filling out registration forms, and lining up transportation and drivers. On the other hand, camps have the effort and expense of building facilities, maintaining them, preparing equipment and activities, and training staff.

Yes, extra effort and cost are required. When Christ left heaven for the cross of Calvary, He set the example of going the extra mile. We ought not to shy away from sacrifice that results in precious souls being saved and lives changed through the preaching and teaching of the Word. Rather than focus on how much extra work camp is, thank the Lord for the opportunity to reach the precious souls He already sacrificed so much to save. Is camp worth it? Yes, IT IS!!!!

The real value of camp must be defined for its eternal, spiritual benefit.

BOTTOM LINE

Camp costs something. Both the extra labor and monetary costs are part of what makes up the price tag of camp. Although it may be difficult to pinpoint the actual market value of a week at camp, one can come up with an accurate idea of camp's value by comparison to other activities or events. Comparing benefits and the associated costs reveal value. But though the question of camp's value is a monetary one, the answer is not a monetary answer. How can one put a price on the worth of a soul?

Churches and families need to understand that camp operations costs are growing and camps struggle to keep them down so people can afford to come to camp. Camps also need to remember that families and churches have to face the ever-increasing camp cost. As camps cut costs without cutting the quality of their ministry, churches can also help address this issue of camp's value by encouraging giving to scholarships and placing camp attendance in perspective in terms families can understand.

To determine the real value of any item, the value equals the benefit divided by the cost. However, when the goal of camp is eternal benefit and that is divided by temporal costs, the quotient is indescribable in value. To gain the proper perspective on camp's value, one need only reflect on how our Lord addressed the priority decisions made between the material and the spiritual. *Matthew 6:33* states, "But seek ye first the kingdom of God, and his righteousness; and all these things shall be added unto you." Equipped with this eternal mindset, one will quickly see that camp's value is eternally defined.

IS CAMP WORTH IT?

One summer I had a young lady that was working with a two-year-old borrowed horse. The horse was pretty wild and I remember the look in the horsemanship camper's eyes was total fear. We backed up into the barn and unloaded the horse right into the round pen. The first time the young lady got into the round pen, the horse was totally jazzy and had one motive—get out of the round pen. The first two days of working with the horse were rough. Then on Wednesday, there was a total change in the horse's attitude. By that night, we were able to put a saddle on the horse and the young lady got on. Thursday morning we taught the horse to load in the trailer. On Thursday afternoon, the owner came and was expecting a fight to load the horse in the trailer. The young lady went to get the horse, haltered him, and walked him out. When I went to take the horse to load him in the trailer, she was crying. I asked what was wrong and she proceeded to tell me this.

"This horse is a lot like I was growing up. I was as wild as he was, doing drugs, living an immoral life style, and stealing. Then God stepped into my life and said, 'Come here. I have something for you.' At first, I refused, but God continued to ask me to step into the middle (like in the round pen) and accept Him as my personal Savior. I accepted Him, and now I am letting God lead me around instead of me doing my own thing."

That Saturday morning during the Shodeo, a huge burly man walked up to me. He told me he was the father of this young lady. He thanked me and gave me a bear hug. The young lady is currently in Bible college. Her mom sent me a two-page letter in a picture frame about the brokenness of Christ and what it means to be submitted to God. I have it hanging in my house.

—Horsemanship Director

CHAPTER EIGHT

Reflections on the Value of Camp

Honesty demands we acknowledge the "Is camp worth it?" question as important. As we face tight budgets and busy calendars, the louder the question becomes. Hearing the same question from church leadership, parents, or others in the congregation demands a serious consideration and a legitimate answer that is more than just, "Well, that is what we have always done!"

In the preface of this book, I mentioned a list I made while serving as a youth pastor (see Appendix A). On the way home from camp each year, I pondered whether or not it was all worth it. As my wife and I discussed it while in that state of tiredness, we seldom came to a positive conclusion. Nevertheless, I would sign a contract with the camp for the next year to reserve the date and place, but I always made sure to include an escape clause I could trigger about half way through the year if I decided to do so. I never did, primarily because I became convinced of, and remain so to this day, that camp is indeed a valuable tool of ministry and well worth the cost.

Yes, it is true that

- the young people had great fun at camp, actually becoming the premier event of the year for them;

- camp provided a life time of memories for them;

- the young people learned all kinds of new activities and skills;

- camp was a well-established tradition at our church;

- camp has positive social aspects;

- camp gave me many opportunities to get to know my young people and spend many hours in conversation with them, setting the basis of relationship for many counseling opportunities during the next year.

But there was more to it than any or all of those reasons, although all those were good reasons and certainly happened each year at camp. The real reasons had to do with the spiritual impact of what happened at camp that made me go back over and over again, no matter how much work it was to get there. **My young people made spiritual decisions at camp that changed their lives, and seeing the results of that heart change kept me going back for more.** Now, do not get me wrong; I do not believe camp did the work. By God's grace, He gave

> " I've been chasing my own dreams and passions lately instead of seeking God . . . but now I remember . . . pursue Christ. What I think is best will end in death.

the increase as the Word was sown in hearts and cultivated by the Holy Spirit. Then it was up to the individual to listen and respond.

Four particular core aspects of the camping methodology provide the environment for that increase from God to sprout in the form of decisions for Him.

Core #1—A Place of Decision

I saw many young people, and even some of the adult sponsors, make decisions everyday as the Word was preached—decisions for salvation, assurance of salvation, full-surrender, and full-time service for the Lord. Decisions were made after invitations and throughout the day as the young people were sought out by their counselors or as they came to me for answers and help. At the end of each week of camp, we had a testimony service, and the young people related to the others what God was doing in their lives. I used their testimonies throughout the next months as springboards to talk with them about the challenges they faced in their lives. As I related this to some of the folks in the church, they wondered what the difference was between preaching at camp and at church; after all, it was the same Word. Now that is true, but the difference is not in the Word, nor the preacher of the Word, but I believe the difference lays in the methodology of camping. Providing a separate setting for the preaching of the Word caused young people to not just hear the words of the preaching, but to really listen to them. The whole idea of the HEART (see chapter 2) of camping is to create an environment where the Word can be focused like a laser on the hearts and minds of the campers.

Core #2—A Place to Consider the Word

The second aspect I will illustrate by relating an experience with a young man in our youth group whom I had prayed for and talked to for over a year. We were at the last Sunday evening service of a two-week revival meeting in our church; the preacher gave a strong

> God gives me everything and every reason to trust Him for everything. I will act upon this knowledge, recommitting my quest to know my God.

message and was now leading the invitation for decisions to be made. The young man was in this service, and I sat two rows behind him; it was obvious he was under great conviction. I determined to talk with him immediately after the invitation if he did not respond in the service. He turned and looked at me, and I saw the emotion in his face and the tear in his eye as the preacher started the closing prayer. I bowed my head to pray for him, and when I looked up he was gone. First I looked in hope toward the front, but he had not gone forward, and I turned to the back to see him exiting the rear door just as the congregation was dismissed. I followed him to the parking lot where I found him in his parents' car with his worldly music playing and the look of concern gone. If any conviction had been in his heart, it seemed to now be dissipated aided by the hard-pounding music.

If this young man had been at camp, the option of easily running to behavior that quenched the Holy Spirit and finding relief from conviction through the noise of the world would not have been easily available. I am convinced one of the key advantages of the camping ministry in these days is the ability to step away from the increasing cultural clutter of noise, activity, media pervasiveness, and busyness of life for a while. Although things are happening at camp, people find it refreshing to change their pace of life and find time to consider the Word of God in relation to their lives. Camp truly does create a place to come apart for a while so those who have ears to hear can hear the Word, and the Holy Spirit can draw them to the Lord Jesus Christ.

Rather than the Spirit being quenched, the camping methodology sets the stage for the stirring up or the fanning of the flames of that convicting voice in one's heart as the Word is sown and watered all week long.

> *But we all, with open face beholding as in a glass the glory of the Lord, are changed into the same image from glory to glory, even as by the Spirit of the Lord. 2 Corinthians 3:18*

Core #3—A Place of Teachable Moments

In the years before I became a full-time youth pastor, I taught high school classes in a Christian school, and one of the things I learned in those few years was how important a teachable moment was to imparting lasting truths to the students. I can remember recognizing such times on occasion and working even harder in those few moments to get across the desired lesson before that moment disappeared. I actually became a student of the teachable moment trying to figure out what they were and what triggered them, so I could encourage such times of "super learning" opportunities more often in my classroom. Sadly, I found such an effort to be harder than I thought, for such moments are difficult to engineer. So while I was teaching I kept my mind open to them, and when I recognized such a time I jumped in with both feet and made as much hay as I could while the sun was shining on their minds!

The term *teachable moment* has been applied by educators to both a physical readiness and a mental readiness to learn. The physical aspect reflects on the fact that a certain level of physical readiness must be present for useful learning to take place. I suppose there is an element of truth to that idea, but in camp work it is not so much the question of being old enough but rather getting too old. According to the Scripture in *Matthew 18:1-14*, there is a time in a child's life when they are more prone to believing in Jesus because pride has not yet fully developed in his life, nor has his heart yet been hardened by sin. So, there is a physical teachable moment in relation to spiritual things, and it appears that within certain obvious limits the younger a child hears and understands the gospel the better, because pride and sin have not yet created a stony heart that resists the gospel and its call to humility. This explains one reason why children's ministries like camps are so important and effective.

The mental readiness aspect to the teachable moment relates to the moment when everything seems to come together at a point in time where the students' interest is high, when their minds are fully engaged on the subject, and when connections are made because they are thinking. Evidences of a teachable moment include a willingness to discuss without arguing, a willingness to ask questions for clarification and more information, and a willingness to listen to the answers with their mind engaged as they accept or receive the truth of the Word of God into their

> " This is a place where you are compelled to examine yourself as the Bible commands. You are constantly confronted with the greatness of our Creator.

hearts. Their eyes sparkle with interest, their memory is enhanced, and their mind is focused on the issue being discussed. Why questions asked in the teachable moment are not why questions that are really saying, "I don't agree with you," but they are why questions that are saying, "I really want to know." Oftentimes the end result of a teachable moment is an act of volition or will that says, "Based on this information I am going to change my life." We call those volitional moments decisions for the Lord Jesus Christ when they are made in response to the preaching and teaching of the truth of God presented in the Scriptures.

The bottom line for me as a youth pastor who had been a teacher was that camp (when the entire HEART of Camping was being applied) was presenting us with more teachable moments each and every day than anything I had ever experienced in working with young people. Because of the consistent opportunities of teachable moments, camp had set the stage for me to have many open doors of ministry, mentoring, and counseling sessions with the young people for the next year. While before I had been nervous about the cost and the work involved in camp, I now was figuring out ways to challenge people to help out with the cost and looking forward with keen anticipation to the next time I could get my young people back to camp.

Core #4—A Place of Eternal Impact

The fourth aspect of the spiritual impact of the camping ministry upon my young people went back full circle to the decisions they made at camp, or even after they left camp, because the Word and the Spirit continued to work in their hearts. Yes, great value comes from seed sown from the Bible preaching and teaching at camp, but the most visible results from camp lay in the harvest of decisions made at camp while the campers were there. I listened to the testimonies of my young people: some received the Lord as their Savior, some surrendered to Him concerning their life choices or behaviors, and some obeyed the Lord by presenting themselves as living sacrifices to Him.

> Wonderful memories with my daughters and very encouraged and spiritually challenged. My life changed due to victories in my perspective of my marriage.

I know that some people would always question the results, saying it was just a mountain-top experience. But the impact on the youth group and individuals was huge, and I could not imagine leading that kind of a spiritual work without using this ministry tool. If I made entertaining the young people and keeping them out of mischief my primary goals, then other choices could be more exciting and fun, with much more variety and certainly more culturally relevance than camp. I was not looking for a material answer to the question, "Is it worth it?"

As I was personally pondering the value of camp, I found that I was now starting to focus on the eternal value of those decisions for the Lord. I began the long process of follow up, mentoring (discipleship), and encouragement necessary for such a huge harvest of decisions for the Lord. I recalled with joy about 75 percent of the campers making some kind of positive decisions for the Lord. Without being too judgmental, I realized with sorrow many of the others also made decisions contrary to the Lord by saying no to His prompting. The rich young ruler of *Luke 18:18–27* turned away from the Lord after hearing His teaching, while Nicodemus turned to Him in new birth in that great passage on salvation found in *John 3*. Even in the Old Testament, Moses (*Deuteronomy 30:19*) and Joshua (*Joshua 24:15*), in addressing the Israelites, preached that God was giving them a choice, and it was their responsibility to choose the right way; their lives and their families would forever be influenced by their decisions.

When the time came around again for me to begin the long and arduous task of planning, organizing, and operating a camp or retreat for the youth or adults of our church, I never said, "This is too much work; I cannot do this again." I realized the spiritual impact and the plenteous harvest, so how could I not do it, regardless of the work! The presentation of the Word of God, the work of the Holy Spirit, and the time of consideration and choices made for the Lord by the campers made the use of the camping methodology (HEART) several times a year an easy decision. The spiritual impact meant the value was there—for all eternity!

BOTTOM LINE

I am convinced to this day, four decades later, God used my questions regarding the labor and cost involved to get my attention and plant the seed in my heart to start a camping ministry for churches of like faith. As a youth pastor, I would have been thrilled if all I had to do was promote camp, raise some funds to cover the excess costs, arrange for transportation, go to camp with the young people, and be free to talk with and minister to the young people without having to worry about all the details. I became involved in the camping ministry so that every church whether large or small could enjoy the benefits of a full-service camping ministry. My hope is that every church has within a reasonable drive this "specialty tool" ready and available as they strive to accomplish their Great Commission.

Because of the teachable moment created by the HEART of camping, the Word of God, and the Holy Spirit, I have found that camp is indeed of great value and eternal benefit, because it is truly a **Place of Decision**!

IS CAMP WORTH IT?

Prayer Chapel journal entry

I came back to camp for just two days this summer, the least time I've spent here for a long time, yet I praise you, Lord, for every minute. Nine summers ago I asked the Lord to use me, told Him I would serve full-time wherever He wanted. Now I am a missionary in Mexico. But it all started here. God, I cannot praise you enough for this place. Year after year as a camper You challenged my heart. Then you gave me two summers of growth as a counselor. I'm so far away (physically) from camp now in a place no one has heard of, working with people whom I don't always understand. But those people are the same as the campers and co-workers I had at camp—people who will matter in eternity, people with souls . . . God, I want to spend and be spent for You.

Letter to camp staff member

Thank you for your vision, concern, and commitment. I made a full commitment to Christ in the summer of 1976, attended Bible college, and now am involved in the Bible publishing ministry at my church. If it wasn't for the structure, yet open environment to worship God in all His glorious surroundings, I don't believe I would be where I am today. It shaped a lot of my growth and the ability to listen for God in the still quiet, although, you wouldn't guess that in all that goes on daily.

APPENDIX A

Planning and Running a Week of Camp

This is a partial list of planning and responsibilities when our church rented a facility and ran our own camp program. The italicized items are those we would do if using a full-service camp.

1. *Travel to the facility for a survey of available activities and options, and take pictures for promotional purposes.*

2. Make all the arrangements with the camp facility—negotiate price, extras, services provided or excluded; agree on dates, get a contract signed, agree on payments, and keep up a running communication with the camp so they did not forget what we decided.

3. *Promote camp to the parents and children, keeping in mind the budget; raise the excess funds needed when we started to exceed the budget (church budgets rarely are able to cover the cost of a properly run camp or retreat).*

4. Design the daily schedule, research, and select the activities.

5. Choose and train the necessary adults to go along as counselors and support team (for both safety and program effectiveness); this required at least a ratio of one adult for every five young people.

6. Collect all the equipment and supplies, print the program booklet with devotional passages, rules, schedule, etc.

7. *Arrange transportation for approximately 200 people to travel over 500 miles away (safety and dependability issues always surfaced).*

8. Arrange for a preacher, get him to and from camp, and provide his travel expenses and love offering.

9. *Secure donations well ahead of time to help supplement the cost of camp.*

10. Plan the extra activities that the camp did not provide to ensure the fun quotient at camp. This included buying and transporting all our own awards as well as printed schedules and devotion booklets for the week.

11. Create a daily schedule fitting the camp's meal times.

12. Spend much time and prayer in planning the spiritual impact upon the young people; camp used as a successful tool is much more vast than a venue for several preaching services a day.

13. Meet with all the adults almost weekly for months in advance to ensure everyone going understands this is not a vacation (although most had to arrange for vacation time from work in order to go); make sure they know how to counsel the young people in matters pertaining to salvation, spiritual growth, full surrender, and consistent Christian walk; make sure their personal testimonies and examples fit their jobs in relation to their camp responsibilities.

14. Supervise and answer questions all day long—usually on very little sleep. This supervision aspect made it difficult for me as the youth pastor to spend counseling time with the young people as I wished I could.

15. Figure out, plan, and practice all the new games and activities to be unveiled at camp.

16. Recruit from the church enough adults to counsel and supervise all the young people, plus 50 percent, because some may experience sickness or job responsibilities. Get them all to take a week of vacation plus pay their own way to camp.

17. Train all those adults in how to counsel young people—prepare the training material, teach the sessions (about six Sunday

afternoons for about two hours each Sunday). Talk to some about not going because they lack leadership at this time or engage them in further training.

18. Work out the budget for the week of camp—travel, extra food at camp (we always had a late night pizza night and a watermelon night), speaker-related costs, extra activities, church staff camp costs, scholarships, booklets, boats, etc.

19. Get someone to lead the music, play the piano, do special music, etc.

20. Plan the skits and special stunts; bring all props needed to camp.

21. Provide extra transportation for my family and me; if I did not arrive early and stay late, the camp would not be ready for us, and the first impression of the campers would hurt the whole week.

22. *Spend more time in prayer.*

Did you note the italicized items? If using a full-service camp, those are the tasks I would do with everything else being performed by the camp ministry. Is it worth it? Absolutely!

APPENDIX B

The Spiritual Punch at Camp

Programs using camp as a platform for preaching have four or five preaching services a day and between services offer familiar activities for young people to enjoy. The vast majority of spiritual decisions happen as a result of preaching services and the subsequent invitations. Small-group based programs such as backpacking trips and adventure camps emphasize the work of the counselor and individual interaction. Christ used a variety of approaches—preaching to large audiences, leading small group discussions (e.g., with His disciples), and talking one-on-one to individuals (e.g., the Samaritan woman); both types of camp programs have their place.

Spiritual purpose and goals should be foremost when camps meld together a platform or small-group based program. Several ways can be used to present the gospel message. Specific programs have additional ones, but the methods listed below are those common to most programs.

1. Personal devotion time—campers read a passage complementing the chapel messages, learn different methods of Bible study, memorize verses, and pray.

2. Examples of counselors and staff—an object lesson in Christian living; our program is designed knowing counselors are put into stressful situations. Using teachable moments, they teach by example how a Christian should act in such situations.

3. Cabin discussion time—practical teaching from God's Word emphasizing, "Why do you believe what you believe?" or, "Why do you do what you do?" This may be an organized time of discussion or a review of the day, becoming a teachable moment.

4. Morning chapel preaching is aimed at the practical aspects of everyday life for that age group.

5. Personal counseling by counselors occurs at various times during the day—usually one-on-one discussions.

   a. Talk to each camper about salvation.

   b. Talk to each camper about the next step on the spiritual ladder, looking for teachable moments and asking questions to open minds and encourage conversation.

6. Cabin activities and structured times.

   a. Cabin devotions—end the day on a spiritual note.

   b. Meal times—song, prayer, conversation, and a verse to meditate on.

7. Challenge courses (e.g., high or low ropes courses)—using teamwork and physical ability, a group tries to meet the objective given by the instructor. After achieving their goal, the group discusses lessons learned and principles illustrated from God's Word.

8. All things—done in a spiritual atmosphere (*1 Corinthians 10:31*).

9. Elimination of worldly influences.

10. Evening service—good, solid, persuasive preaching from God's Word.

    a. Emphasis on salvation, full surrender, and obedience to God's Word.

    b. Invitation given; opportunity given for decisions and one-on-one counseling.

    c. Campfire or testimony time—an opportunity for the camper to share with his cabin or all the campers what God has worked in his life.

11. Constant testimony of God's limitless creation.

APPENDIX C

Promoting Camp by Communicating Value

Practical Suggestion: When promoting camp each year, include with the announcement a quick, verbal reminder of the number of decisions made in previous years at camp. Remind the people how the Lord provided financially for camp the previous year through scholarships and other methods. A pastor or youth pastor sharing his own camp story and the decisions he made during his youth is helpful.

The following list is also helpful to the decision makers. Maybe read two each week during the time of promotion and registration or insert in the bulletin.

1. Camp is a special place that results in a harvest of decisions for Christ.

2. Camp location provides isolation from worldly offenses.

3. Camp brings campers back to nature and creation and thus back to God.

4. Camp staff provide a godly example.

5. Camp reinforces, not undermines, the local church's positions and teaching.

6. Camp is a place of spiritual saturation. The Word of God is constantly being taught with authority, persuasion, and biblical content not only on the platform by the preacher but also throughout the day by staff members and church sponsors.

7. Camp has a planned program geared to each age group and aimed at accomplishing specific goals and objectives.

8. Camp counselors, year-round staff, and campers band together in prayer for the salvation of unbelieving campers.

9. Camp is a new environment. Young people can leave their old reputations behind them.

10. Decisions are made at camp; discipleship continues at church.

APPENDIX D

Camp is a Place of Decision
for salvation, full surrender, and consistent Christian walk.

The four simple principles expanded give counselors more direction in helping their campers.

Step One—Identification with God

1. Believe on the Lord for salvation—*Romans 10:9–10, 13*

2. Tell others—*Matthew 10:32; Romans 10:11*

3. Baptism—*Acts 2:41*

Step Two—Fellowship with God *1 John 1:5–9*

1. Bible study—*1 Peter 2:2; Joshua 1:8*

2. Prayer—*John 16:24*

3. Sin confessed—*1 John 1:9*

Step Three—Decision to Become Pleasing to God

1. Willing to do God's will by obeying the Bible—*1 Samuel 15; Hebrews 13:20–21*

2. Decision for full surrender to doing God's will in life—*Romans 12:1–2*

Step Four—Transformed Life: A Continuing Process
Romans 12:2

1. Conforming to God

    a. Change at salvation—*2 Corinthians 5:17*

    b. Spiritual growth—*1 Peter 2:2; 2 Timothy 3:16–17*

    c. His workmanship—*Ephesians 2:10*

    d. Fruits of the Spirit—*Galatians 5:22–23*

2. Developing convictions based on God's Word—*not a definitive list*

    a. Friends—*Ephesians 5:11; 2 Thessalonians 3:6, 14; 1 Corinthians 15:33; Proverbs 13:20*

    b. Talk—*Ephesians 4:29*

    c. Attitude—*Philippians 2:5, 14*

    d. Money—*1 Timothy 6:6–11; Luke 6:38*

    e. Sex—*1 Thessalonians 4:3–8*

    f. Life goals and motives—*Matthew 6:33*

APPENDIX E

Four Parts of Counseling at Camp

What is a counselor? A biblical counselor is a committed, maturing believer who is trained to apply biblical principles to deal with the problems of everyday living. **The Bible must be our foundation and tool in all counseling** *(Psalm 1; Ecclesiastes 12:13–14; 2 Timothy 3:16–17)*. Biblical counseling has four components. Every component is important!

1. **Understand the problem**—*Proverbs 18:13; James 1:19*

   a. Ask questions

   b. Make observations

2. **Give hope from God's Word**—*1 John 1:9; 1 Corinthians 10:13; Hebrews 4:15–16*

3. **Present the decision**—*Romans 6:6–7, 12–13; Philippians 4:6–9*

   a. During invitation

   b. One-on-one conversations

   c. Sin confessed—*1 John 1:9*

4. **Develop a plan**—*Romans 12:1–2; James 1:22–25*

   a. During invitation

   b. One-on-one conversations

APPENDIX F

Survey on Evangelism of Teenagers

Have you ever wondered what factors in teenagers' lives God uses to draw them to faith in Christ? We asked! Following are some of the findings of a special study.—Editor's Note

Survey among students who would describe themselves as "followers of Christ within the past two years" [during or after 2003]. Asked the following open-ended question: Tell me everything you can remember about your experience of first choosing to become a follower of Jesus Christ.

See more information on study at website:

www.youthworkers.net/pdf/NetMag-Spring2006_9.pdf

Most-mentioned influences in becoming a Christian:

1. Church Camp/Retreat/Special Event/Conferences (DEFAULT when unspecified camp experience is mentioned)

2. Personal (Internal) Turmoil

3. Friends—Non-verbal (DEFAULT when friends are mentioned; e.g., caring, accepting, example, presence)

4. Specific Challenge to Act

5. Attending Church

6. Friends—Verbal (e.g., inviting, counseling, challenging, coaching)

7. Church Youth Ministry Involvement

8. Parents

9. Parachurch Youth Ministry Involvement

10. Youth Leader(s)—Verbal (e.g., inviting, counseling, challenging, coaching)

11. Other Family Members

12. Youth Leader(s)—Non-verbal (DEFAULT when youth leaders are mentioned; e.g., caring, accepting, example, presence)

13. Family Stress / Crisis / Divorce

14. Dating Relationships

15. Parachurch Camp / Retreat / Special Event / Conferences

16. Other

17. External Crises

18. Other Adult Church Leader(s)

> *"First, it makes sense to equip Christian teenagers to articulate their faith to their non-Christian friends. Our analysis showed that teenagers with little or no religious background are especially responsive to this sort of verbal outreach from friends.*
>
> *Next, make use of camps, retreats, or conferences when it comes to evangelism. We found that such events are most important for the conversions of teenagers with little or no religious background. They are also very effective when they include a "specific challenge to act." And, for whatever reason, these pointed invitations to begin a relationship with Christ are especially significant when trying to evangelize males. My final suggestion is to blend the first two. Focus some energy on equipping Christian teenagers to invite their non-Christian friends to camps, retreats, or conferences. It's a different kind of verbal coaching, but it seems to pay off, especially on those teens coming from less religious backgrounds."* –Dave Rahn, author of above article

10699209R00071

Made in the USA
San Bernardino, CA
06 December 2018